BOW AND ARROW WAR

BOW AND ARROW WAR

From FANY to Radar in World War II

Marjorie Inkster

LARGE PRINT

Oxford

First published in Great Britain 2005
by
Brewin Books Ltd.

Published in Large Print 2008 by ISIS Publishing Ltd.,
7 Centremead, Osney Mead, Oxford OX2 0ES
by arrangement with
Brewin Books Ltd.

British Library Cataloguing in Publication Data
Inkster, Marjorie
     Bow and arrow war. – Large print ed.
     (Isis reminiscence series)
     1. Inkster, Marjorie
     2. Great Britain. Army. Royal Electrical and
     Mechanical Engineers – Officers – Biography
     3. Military engineers – Great Britain – Biography
     4. Women engineers – Great Britain – Biography
     5. World War, 1939–1945 – Personal narratives,
     British
     6. Large type books
     I. Title
     940.5'41241'092

ISBN 978–0–7531–9498–0 (hb)
ISBN 978–0–7531–9499–7 (pb)

Printed and bound in Great Britain by
T. J. International Ltd., Padstow, Cornwall

Contents

QUOTATION FROM
THE RED BOOK ABOUT RADAR
(Army Radar. War Office 1950)

"This novel device that grew so rapidly was of an intricate nature that was almost unknown to all but a very few scientific and technical personnel at the time that the first supplies were reaching operational units. It included many components and appliances previously unknown outside laboratories and the equipments contained upwards of a hundred valves, thousands of radio components, several cathode ray tubes and complicated and delicate gearing and other mechanical aids. It presented new problems in training personnel of all grades, in devising the essential methods of test, in the technique of maintenance and in the development of new forms of testing apparatus. The provision of detailed instructional and technical pamphlets, as well as special means of store holding, parts lists and new methods of packaging for transport, shipping and handling had also to be initiated."

ACKNOWLEDGMENTS

My first thanks are due to Martyn Clark of the REME Museum at Arborfield. A Brigadier (retired) with a warm, friendly voice answered the telephone when I rang about three years ago. Martyn came up with various helpful leads and small documents against which I could check my memories. The Museum photographic department also helped greatly.

Next comes Sue Casson who started me off with the book — a skilled computer operator to whom I dictated at first. When Sue got a full-time job and was unable to continue working for me, I ran to our dear Bampton librarian, Jan, for advice. Michael Pelham overheard my anguished cries in the library, whipped out his mobile and produced Sally Nicoll for me.

How can I thank Sally enough! She is a very efficient secretary, a wizard with the computer. For an hour a week she has helped me sort out my memories of wartime days as they surfaced somewhat haphazardly. She has organised me, prodded me, soothed me and encouraged me. I am grateful for her patience, efficiency, mind reading ability and enthusiasm without which this little book would never have been completed.

Thank you to Chris Ruck for reading my manuscript fairly early on and taking the trouble to write such useful comments although I gathered he did not anticipate that the book would ever be published!

I thank all my friends for egging me on and bearing with my tendency to live in the period 1940–46 at intervals over the last three years.

Finally, thank you, of course, to Alan Brewin my publisher for taking on such an unknown quantity and explaining publishing procedure so patiently to a beginner.

INTRODUCTION

Although I do not feel it, I am well past my sell-by date, or to change the metaphor a bit, I am an antique recently chipped a bit round the edges.

The period 1940–46 is a very small portion of my life — one patch in a large and colourful patchwork quilt. One of my friends said on the telephone the other day that perhaps I thought of it as the happiest part of my life. I was surprised. It certainly was not that. I was later to have a University life, a Chaplaincy life, a Psychotherapy life, a Church Ministry and a long Social Services life. One might say "Jill of all trades and mistress of none". The years of the war were intensely interesting technically and full of challenge. We had the conviction that we were contributing something very worthwhile to the war effort. But apart from the many friendships and laughter on the gun sites they were, in terms of my social and intellectual life, extremely uneventful.

I feel the need to write about what it was like to work on radar during the war, because no one else has, as far as I know. And in all that I have read about AA Command, no one has even mentioned that women were working on the technical side.

I have never kept a diary since childhood. Too busy? Too lazy? My memory must have failed me often in this book: but there are not many people left now who can contradict me!!

CHAPTER
ONE

Beginning with the FANY

The Battle of Britain period was the time I did my basic training in the FANY. We were housed in Pinewood, near Camberley and practised drill on a sunny parade ground. Often there were dogfights going on overhead with vapour trails in the sky and shrapnel in the bushes. Once, as we went in to tea, a plane with German markings swooped down over the house, low enough for us to see the pilot. I remember endless first aid training and itchy shirts (how they itched!) under hot tunics, under heavy gas masks hung with tin hats. We all painted our tin hats with FANY. badges in red and that emblem on my hat followed me right through subsequent adventures for the rest of the war.

Once or twice some of us went to The Pantiles for tea. We were not to know it, but this was the restaurant where Douglas Bader met his future wife — a romantic spot indeed.

FANYs were not at all militaristic at the time, but strict on basic drill and marching. Hence the appearance of Sergeant Major Brand from Sandhurst to lick us into shape before passing out. His voice was what the French would call "formidable" like a foghorn in the Mersey. The enormous bellow with which he delivered commands ended with an extraordinary squeak which I never heard before or since. We were proud to have our passing out parade at Sandhurst.

Soon after I was posted to 6th Western Motor Company, Chester, we moved into a new requisitioned house by the river Dee — Dee Hills Park. Bedding was brought in for us from army supplies. When I say "bedding", I do not mean anything as grand as sheets or pillowcases. Just blankets. Horrible dark brown blankets. Horrible coarse scratchy blankets. And — horrors! — blankets with fleas in them! Those blankets were returned to stores p.d.q. (and the person responsible for issuing them, I hope, got a flea in his ear).

There were one or two smallish raids on Chester. During one of them, we found that an incendiary bomb had come through our roof and lodged in the loft. One brave FANY climbed a ladder into the loft and we handed buckets of sand up to her to put on the bomb and put out the flames. The incendiary was not easily extinguished and soon we were running out of sand. A resourceful corporal rushed into the garden and started filling a bucket with earth. She was digging frantically when a pompous air raid warden came up the path and said, "Do you know you've got an incendiary in your roof?" She said scathingly, "What do you think I am digging in the garden for at two in the morning?" "Well anyway," he said, unabashed, "we'll come and put it out for you". "Oh no you won't, thank you," she said forcefully, "It's our incendiary." So it was put out by the FANYs.

During my time with the FANY (6th Western Motor Company) in Chester, I had a very strange experience. I encountered a "change of sex" situation at a time when I had never even heard of such a thing. Two of my friends and I got to know a small FANY sergeant with an Eton crop called Jo. This very boyish looking character turned out to be a boy indeed. His or her story centred round undescended testicles in the early years of life so Jo was brought up as a girl. Exactly what stage things had reached when Jo joined the FANY we never discovered but somehow "she" managed to pass the initial medical examination.

In our innocence we thought of Jo as a rather eccentric, boyish little FANY who was a really brilliant ballroom dancer and taught us to tango and do a slow foxtrot. Those two dances always remained my favourites, because they were the only two in which I had received expert tuition. Another FANY, Joyce W, got married at her home in Pinner, Middlesex and several of us were invited to the wedding. Jo was one of the guests. The bride's father watched Jo intently and towards the end of the party passed a comment to two of us that there was something distinctly odd about "her" sexuality. It was fairly soon after the wedding that Jo confided in us. I cannot remember the timing very well, but I think I went off on my radar training fairly soon after this. Some years afterwards, I saw an article about Jo R and change of sex in the Sunday Express. No mention was made of the FANY period of Jo's life, but I seem to remember that the Express spoke of his having got married.

This must have happened roughly at the same time as the Liverpool raids, which were long lasting, violent and destructive. In the spring of 1941 Admiral Erich Raeder wrote a memo to the Führer of the German Reich, Adolf Hitler. It said: "An early concentrated attack on Britain is necessary, on Liverpool for example, so that the whole nation will feel the effect." (From "Three Women of Liverpool" by Helen Forrester) My home was at Heswall, on the Wirral peninsular which lies between Dee and Mersey. Heswall was on the Dee. My parents grew used to the air raid warnings for Liverpool, and after a while stayed in bed when they sounded, because the bombs were falling quite a distance away. I had had flu in Chester and the FANYs gave me 48 hours sick leave, so I hitch-hiked home to Heswall. When I got there, I discovered to my surprise that my very unjittery mother had spent the whole of the previous day gathering together our most precious possessions from all over the house and putting them in a very large solid oak Elizabethan court cupboard in the dining room. She was a highlander and clairvoyant: had a premonition of what was about to happen to us.

We went to bed as usual, but about 1am the air raid warning went. I snuggled down in bed, but my mother came in and in spite of my protests dug me out of bed. Two evacuated sisters, who had been bombed out of their house in Liverpool, were billeted with my parents. My mother dug them out of bed, too. Hardly had we all

4

assembled downstairs, when the house fell in on us. We had had a direct hit by a 1,000 lb bomb. You never hear the bomb that hits you. One of the two sisters died at my feet with horrible choking noises which I shall remember for the rest of my life.

I could hear my father calling to see if we were all right. It turned out that he had been thrown clear and was lying with a beam across his middle, gazing up at the stars. My mother answered in a low voice and I could stretch out my hand and touch her hair. I put my hands up and found I was in a sort of coffin of planks and rubble but with plenty of air. Almost immediately we heard the blessed voices of rescuers, air raid wardens and other trained staff. They located us by our shouts and found that I was lying in the hall against the dining room wall which was still standing. They made a hole in the wall and passed me a torch. Oh, the relief of the light! But the relief was short-lived because I then saw my mother's situation. A great beam had come from above and lodged, end on, in her back, knocking her head-downwards, with her knees up under her, so that she could scarcely breathe. How could they possibly get her out?

The men got me out through the hole in the wall and lifted me onto somebody's back. My slippers stayed behind in the hole and there was broken glass everywhere. My father had been freed and was sitting nearby, but they wanted me out of the way so that they could rescue my mother. I was piggy-backed to a nearby friend's house. Then, thank God, my father remembered that my brother Fraser had fixed up an extension in the drawing room from the "wireless" in the dining room. Fraser had got into the foundations of the house which were about five feet deep. Quickly the rescuers found a way into them. They located the spot under where my mother was trapped, made a hole, lowered her into the foundations on to a stretcher and carried her out. They got her out in the nick of time as the doctors said later she was breathing only with the top of one lung.

My darling mother was taken overnight to the Children's Hospital and then next morning to a delightful little private nursing home nearby. I went to visit her that morning and the matron warned me not to react too badly to her appearance. She was propped up in bed and greeted me with a lovely smile. The smile was in a face which was entirely black, with tiny burst capillaries and eyes whose whites were completely scarlet. I was glad I had been warned. During the next few months she was to make a complete recovery.

Looking back on the night of the bombing, I recall a strange mixture of sensations. As background, there was the terrified howling of our lovely black cocker spaniel: the noise of our evacuee dying: the horror of seeing how my mother was trapped: the stench of old plaster in the ruins of the house: the relief of the first torchlight. But remaining with me ever since is the memory of a sustaining presence. The nearest description I can give is that of a hand in mine — not literally feeling like a hand, but having the effect of a hand — the hand of God in kindness and comfort. It was a quite profound religious experience which I have

6

never attempted to describe or explain to anyone before this.

The morning after the raid, I rang Clare Fell, the adjutant in my FANY company and was given a week of what was called "bombed leave". My father was in bed for a week with a bad back, so I had to deal with the situation at what used to be "home"! The bomb had been a thousand-pounder and had made a direct hit. There were a couple of half-walls standing in the front of the house, so there were bits of furniture, books and even pictures to be rescued almost immediately. A grandfather clock emerged almost intact: also a pair of Japanese porcelain pictures with a long and romantic family history. In front of the house was erected a large notice saying, "The penalty of looting is death". In the middle of what had been the hall was the telephone, still ringing when our number was dialled, so people who did not know about our bomb wondered why we never answered.

That first morning was weird. Having been carried in my nightie to a friend's house, I emerged without a single possession. I had no soap, toothbrush, sponge, shoes, underclothes or top clothes. I discovered that because they were Government property, my tin hat, uniform and gasmask had been taken to the local police station and I had to walk there, about a mile, to collect them, in borrowed clothing, doing some shopping on the way (with borrowed money of course)! After a week of supervising the digging out of various treasures, including family silver, and finding temporary repositories for them all, I returned to Chester and Brenda, my sister, took over.

Each night in bed I recalled every detail of the bombing night. I allowed all my feelings of fear and horror to surface each time and then went to sleep. This process went on for weeks, until I "worked it out of my system" and developed sensations rather like boredom. I knew little about psychology at the time but automatically developed this technique which I much later discovered was the best possible one for dealing with great trauma.

Because I was not old enough to drive (FANY drivers had to be 20), I was put on to petrol accounting. FANY had numerous staff cars in Chester and ambulances all over Cheshire, Lancashire, North Wales and the Isle of Man. Drivers had to complete a work ticket every day, detailing speedometer reading (start and finish), petrol in tank (start and finish). Some FANYs were very good, others not so good. Every two months or so I had to take all the piles of work tickets to the Army Auditor. I regret to say I was responsible for a good deal of forgery to make sums on the work tickets come out right. The Auditor was very understanding.

CHAPTER
TWO

Radar Training

After a while the situation palled. Then suddenly there was a circular asking for volunteers to be trained as radio mechanics (later known as radar mechanics). I think I imagined myself working in communication with glamorous RAF pilots, so I said, "Yes please". In no time at all, I was whisked up to London to do a three months basic training in wireless and generators. We were all girls together, about forty of us. We worked at the Regent Street Polytechnic and did some workshop training too, learning to solder and braise and use micrometers, file and use a lathe and make tools such as flat spanners, box spanners and set squares. ("I'm the girl that makes the thing that holds the thingamabob!!" Gracie Fields) We were taught all these things by a little bald-headed man who was scrupulously polite and rather fatherly. He was so polite that it was not until our last session with him that he plucked up courage to reveal the name of the middle-sized file we were taught to use. It was a BASTARD file.

Our accommodation was in Montagu Square, off Baker Street and conditions were pretty appalling.

Several houses in the square had been bombed, but ours was intact. We had an orderly who was supposed to keep the fire alight in the range which heated the boiler in the basement. This was for our central heating and hot water supply. Well, she did not. We used to sneak down in the evenings to try to remedy the situation, but more often than not the water was cold and so were the radiators. We slept in two-tier bunks, with army biscuits (mattress in three sections). We had nowhere to keep our clothes and possessions except in our kit bags. If we wanted to study in the evenings, which we needed to do to keep up with material which was being crammed into us, we had to go up to the attics, where presumably pre-war maid-servants slept. There we sat to study at army trestle tables with our army greatcoats on and gloves. There was no heating and this was the period October to December.

Long before dawn cracked, we were up and dressed, with buttons polished. We had no battle dress. We lined up in the road outside and stood to be inspected by a fearsome ATS sergeant. First she looked at the buttons on our greatcoats and then we had to open them so that she could inspect our tunic buttons. It was pitch dark so she had to use a torch. Occasionally we had respirator drill. The first time we had this was hilarious. At the command "One, we slid our gas mask cases round onto our chests. At the command "Two" we put our right hands on the fastenings on top of the equipment. At "Three" we pulled the case open. That was the moment! Things sprang out of those cases, which were not part of the respirators. There were lipsticks, powder compacts, pens and pencils, eyebrow tweezers, cigarette packets, cough sweets, and combs.

Then came the march to breakfast, which was at the Regent Street Polytechnic. We had a storm lantern fore and aft. The journey was quite hazardous in the dark but luckily there was little traffic. Some mornings that year the fog was so thick we could scarcely see where we were going. It was "Left, left, left, right, left" all the way. The route we took was partly along Wigmore Street, but it was quite a long way to have to march before breakfast.

We were allowed out in the evenings when we were not studying. The sergeant sat in the hall and made sure our passes were in order. My friend Marian Bridgman was a keen skater and I wanted to learn, so we planned to have an evening at the Queen's Club. I had not been issued with trousers in the FANY, but Marian had been given them in her previous job. She and I came downstairs from our sleeping quarters with our greatcoats on. Sergeant W immediately called out, "Bridgman!" We went over to her. "You've got trousers on. You know you are not allowed out like that. Go back and change immediately." Marian retreated upstairs and after a few minutes reappeared with stockinged legs showing beneath her coat. Actually, all she had done was roll up her trouser legs. However, she got away with it. One up to us!

Another time I went to a party in my FANY uniform. Coming back, our transport ran out of petrol and we had to walk. We arrived back about twenty minutes after the deadline set by our passes. Our charming sergeant was sitting in the hall waiting for us. She was fuming! She was so set on dishing out our punishment, whatever it was, that she never noticed what I was wearing. I was in full FANY gear, with beautiful barathea tunic and skirt, Sam Brown and all. I could not believe my luck and retreated upstairs to bed with all speed.

It was so exciting! Having spent three months in Montagu Square and Regent Street sweating away at our basic radio theory, after Christmas, in January 1942 our class of thirty girls went up to Gainsborough in Lincolnshire. We were at last going to see the secret radar equipment. Remember that no one at that time outside a small group knew anything about radar. So it was a great adventure we were embarking on. Gainsborough was a small town of many dark little houses, with several rather homely pubs and I think about thirty fish and chip shops. The girls who were taking the radar course were all billeted in private homes. Mine was a not very wealthy home, with an old-fashioned parlour, only used on Sundays; but my hosts received me kindly and made me very comfortable in my bedroom. In the army, I was not used to having a luxurious mattress and gorgeous, large, fluffy, artificial silk down quilt.

We needed a bit of comfort at night because conditions in the radar school were pretty spartan. The weather was incredibly cold and wet. Although the girls had the advantage of being billeted in civilian homes, while the men lived in a rather run-down camp, we all together had to endure lecture-rooms which were primitive in the extreme. I vividly recall sitting in a Nissen hut, with greatcoat and gloves while snow actually drifted down onto us through holes in the metal roof. Where it settled on the floor it did not melt because the hut was so cold. Our hands were red and swollen with chilblains and we all had terrible colds and coughs, but we were extraordinarily happy. I have some very jolly photographs of a crowd of us snowballing each other.

I found the radar course absolutely enthralling. I can recall my first glimpse of the inside of the transmitter cabin, with its strange and exciting ozone smell. There was the hum of the blower motor, keeping the huge BT98 transmitter valves cool. I can remember being warned about what then seemed to be a very large voltage on the TX valves and told how to ensure that it had bled away through the resister circuit, before we touched the BT98s. The staff sergeant demonstrated the earthing stick which was a safety measure and we were invited to try what happened if the voltage was still on the valve. I was not daunted by high voltages, only by loud bangs from guns, which I encountered later on the gun sites.

As far as I can remember, all the lecturing and practical instruction was given to us by staff sergeants, who had three stripes with a crown above them. These were highly intelligent men with an extensive background in electronics. They were very good teachers and nearly all had an excellent sense of humour, which helped. Some were very good-looking too and I fell for them a little — or with one or two a lot! Alas, we did not see them "out of hours" so there was no chance of a real relationship developing.

I cannot recall where we did our studying but I know we worked very hard and discussed with each other. A little bit of folklore developed among the girls. At school we had circulated a rumour that if a girl sat for long on a hot radiator, she got piles. On the Gainsborough course, a rumour went round that girls who worked on radar became infertile. That worried us a little.

I seem to remember we had a fair amount of time for study during the day, because I do recall that we had quite a lot of fun in the evenings. It was not the sort of fun I would have had at home if there had not been a war, but it catered very well for our high spirits in 1941 (when I was aged twenty). A good deal of our time was spent in the pubs: but we tried out a good many of the pubs in turn. About the furthest away was the "Crooked Billet", at the far end of the town. The main object of the exercise was certainly not what the young now call "binge drinking". We liked being together — about ten of us — mixed men and girls. We liked being in a nice warm pub. The girls probably had two very watery half pints during the evening and the men probably two pints each. We laughed and talked, but above all we sang. We sang our hearts out. We paired off to some extent but there was little if anything of what you would call romance, except for one couple. One or two of the men were married. One was engaged to a girl in another service. I had a boyfriend who wanted to get romantic, but I didn't. We proved that it was possible to have friendships between the sexes without jumping into bed with each other.

The couple who did go the "whole hog" were a not very intelligent, rather giggly, bright-eyed little person and a man whom I thought not in the least attractive. He was an Aberdonian and turned out to be married, though he kept it dark while in Gainsborough. Of course, in our little gang we all knew what was going on and we were worried about our small friend. Remember there were no contraceptive pills at the time and the other methods, such as French Letters, were not all that reliable. We did not trust Ian and were afraid that the silly girl would get herself pregnant. Post-war girls and older women will find it difficult to believe — but we were all *sorry* for her!!

It was decided that someone should try to appeal to Ian to "lay off". I thought I might have a go at it. During a local dance I got hold of Ian and said, "I want to talk to you about something." We agreed to go outside, so into the pitch dark we went, just to one side of the main door. I began, "You are just not being fair to Kay . . ." He replied, "So that's what it's all about, is it?" in an arrogant sort of way. He grabbed my hand and said, "Touch it." "It" turned out to be his erect penis! This was my first experience of touching such an object and I did not want to start with Ian. I wasn't even tempted. I shouted angrily, "That's a damned cheek and really nasty of you. Get away from me." I shot back into the dance hall and a minute later Ian came back in looking rather surprised. I was surprised too, as I had never before encountered such extraordinary masculine behaviour: had found it very, very embarrassing and never discussed it with anyone in our group of friends.

One of the highlights of the Gainsborough course was the hospitality and help we got from a local couple called the Blighs. The Blighs lived in a not very large house with a front room into which they invited our little gang of ten, each Sunday evening. We could hardly believe their generosity. They thought we needed a change from pubs and we loved the homely atmosphere. We brought with us a large box of buns or cakes and they supplied tea and milk. All that happened was chat and song.

> "Old Casey would waltz with the strawberry blonde"
> "Red sails in the sunset"
> "Hutsut Rawlston on the Riller, And a Brawla Brawla Sooit" (in Norwegian)
> "Don't sit under the apple tree with anyone else but me"
> "Smoke gets in your eyes"
> "She'll be coming round the mountain when she comes"
> "The nightingale sang in Berkley Square"
> "Begin the Beguin"
> "You are my sunshine"
> "White cliffs of Dover"

The noise must have been considerable. Looking back over the years, my friend Marian and I wonder how much the neighbours suffered. We never gave it a thought.

Another form of entertainment was a cinema, where hungry mortals could get some extra nourishment in the cinema café, if one got there before food ran out. Generally the early supper there was beans on toast, or — beans on toast.

There were unit dances with quite lively bands and proper ballroom dancing which I loved. There were talks. There were snowballing fights, to keep us warm. There were the fish and chip shops and very good they were.

After an evening's singsong at a pub, we used to line up across the road, link arms and bellow our songs all the way home. By the standards of early forties, it was pretty bad behaviour. A very pleasant older male student ticked us off gently for being so noisy. I don't think it affected us very much. We were full of *joie de vivre* and needed to let off steam. Getting near home, we divided up, but our boys would not have thought of not seeing us home to our billets.

Lord of all eagerness, Lord of all faith,
Whose strong hands were skilled at the plane and
 lathe,
Be there at our labours and give us, we pray,
Your strength in our hearts, Lord, at the noon of
 the day.

CHAPTER
THREE

Greenford Ordnance Depot

When we finished the Gainsborough course, the girls did very well in the final examinations. The authorities did not ask us where we wanted to be posted. The girls all went together in a batch to the Royal Ordnance Depot at Greenford. We were to work on fourth line maintenance, which I will explain later.

The truck which collected us from the railway station dropped three of us at a suburban-looking house not far from the depot. We were told it was a temporary billet. A rather sleazy-looking woman took us upstairs and into a bedroom. There was what used to be called a camp bed in the corner, another narrow bed along a wall and a third semi-double bed. There was hardly room to move, but we tossed for the bigger bed, thinking we wouldn't be staying in that house anyway. The whole place smelled fusty and the reason soon emerged when our landlady showed us round. There were baby chickens in the dining room — about twenty of them — and there were three very large dogs, unwashed and smelly, which lived in the house.

We washed and got out into the fresh air as quickly as we could and down the road to a forces' canteen, which we had been told about, where we got some supper. We stayed out until the last possible moment. When we returned and went upstairs to what we thought was "our" bedroom we got a surprise. The landlady's daughter sat up in the camp bed. When the three of us recovered from the shock, we realised it was too late to do anything about it that night, so we must have done an "eeny, meeny, miney, mo" to settle who should share the very narrow double bed. I know I was one of the unlucky ones and the weather was very hot. It was actually against King's Regulations for two girls to sleep in the same bed, so we made a fuss the next morning and we were all moved. This incident was a bit of a warning of what was to come for us at a depot which was badly run and whose senior officers seemed to disregard the welfare of the other ranks. We were not daunted, however, because we were a resilient lot, proud of our jobs, looking forward to using our technical training and keen to learn more. We respected our radar teachers and were disrespectful to our ATS sergeants and corporals who belonged to the depot.

These objectionable people took great pleasure in acting exactly like the caricatures of NCOs one saw in newspapers. The sergeant who had most to do with us was possessed of an enormous bosom, strangely shaped legs and a shrill and strident voice. The trouble was that the powers-that-be had decreed that our group of radar mechanics had to be marched everywhere in columns of three. Especially this applied to meals. The sergeant would come to the radar workshop hangar ages before our mealtimes were due. She fell us in and marched us down to the other ranks' mess long before we were allowed to go in to eat. We stood "at ease" in the glaring sun waiting in our ranks for twenty minutes or more. There was no shirtsleeve order at the time and we stewed.

We found ways of taking revenge. Once, I remember, we were being marched along the main street of the depot and had to avoid something coming the other way, so we were given "right incline". We pretended not to hear the next order, which would have put us in a straight line again. We just went on "right inclining" and carefully wrapped ourselves round a lamp-post. We all kept our faces straight, but the sergeant went purple in the face and utterly failed to straighten us out, so we fell out in disorder.

The food when we got it was disgusting! The meat was gristly and unchewable and tasted bad. One day someone at my table found half a mouse in a jam roll and took it to the orderly officer. Someone on the other side of the dining hall eventually turned up with the other half-mouse. It was a wonder we did not all die of food poisoning. After we left Greenford, we heard that the officer in charge of messing was court-martialled for stealing thousands of pounds worth of government food.

The radar mechanics stood up for ourselves, demanding better conditions and did succeed in meeting the Commanding Officer. Things improved a little, but Colonel Johnson-Davies was far too full of his own importance to care very much about what happened to his troops. The ordnance depot was a huge place, almost like a small town with a railway line running across one end. There was a main street, with several side streets running off it. These were named Portal Place, Pile Avenue, Alexander Square, but the main road was named Johnson-Davies Street.

None of these conditions daunted us at all. The fourth line maintenance work we were doing was an excellent part of our training and development as radar mechanics. Radar sets and radio equipment were sent to the depot because they were completely beyond local repair. Some from the south coast had been machine-gunned or had been near an explosion of some kind or had been set on fire. Sometimes there were massive blood stains on the floor of the cabin. They needed stripping down and often required almost complete rebuilding. So we learnt, under one or two extremely good and pleasant NCOs, to read the circuit diagrams and blue prints, to make new switches and re-wire complete circuits. We learnt far more about the "innards" of the equipment than we could ever have learned on a gun site. We took our jobs very seriously, but we had a lot of fun.

One day a reporter from one of the Sunday broadsheets came to see us. He picked out three of us for a photograph and wanted us pushing a trolley. We said indignantly that we never pushed trolleys but he insisted it would make a good photograph. He loaded some crates with huge transmitter valves onto the platform. We did not notice until the photos came out that the crates were upside down labelled "This Way Up With Care". This offended our pride.

We were working not only on the Mark II radars, on which we had been trained, but also on CD/CHL — Coastal Defence Chain Home Low — which were stationed on the coast to give early warning to Army and Royal Airforce. I did not like the CD/CHL much, because it was black and tinny, not manufactured by Cossor. Our Mark II radar was Cossor-made, pearl grey and solid and clean looking.

We worked long hours. There was always a shortage of radar sets in the country and the need for them on the gun sites was great. Production of these very complex pieces of equipment could never be sufficient. At one point, we were working a full six-day week and nearly sixty hours a week. However, willing as we were, at that point our "production" deteriorated and the powers that be had to reduce our weekly total of hours. I do remember we did not get our 48-hour leaves which all personnel were entitled to and for months we had not had the normal annual allowance of leave. But we were young and healthy and I do not remember feeling unduly tired.

Not long before we were posted from Greenford I was informed one day that I was on a "cadre" course. What this could be I did not know, but eventually discovered that it was a course for potential ATS NCOs. It was tough, but interesting. We learnt all about fire equipment: how to find the fire hydrants and how to unroll the hoses: how to connect the sections of hose together and turn on the pressure. Everything was heavy and surprisingly hard work. Then there were lessons in another kind of fire control. They gave us rifles and taught us about the various parts of them. We were to go on to firing them and I was very apprehensive. In fact, "scared" would be a better word: was convinced that when the time came the thing would blow up in my face. Luckily, before we got to that stage, word came through that rifle practice for girls was to be discontinued.

On the NCOs course we did a lot of drill. The sergeant in charge of the course was a man and he enjoyed being sarcastic. Because of the FANY flashes on my jacket, he christened me "Mobile" — "Hi, Mobile, what do you think you are doing?" I got the feeling that it was a sort of game and grinned happily back at him. I noticed that when a girl looked frightened, he got quite nasty with her. People who are inclined to bully get like that. I am sure this is why some poor army recruits have such a bad time of it.

Shortly before we left Greenford, we were told that an exhibition squad of ATS from another unit were to put on some demonstrative marching for us. "Oh, God!" we thought. "How boring!" But it was a revelation to me. I remembered how much I had enjoyed learning to march at Camberley when I first joined the FANY and these girls obviously enjoyed giving their demonstration at Greenford. Marching like that, in various formations, is an experience unlike anything else. The feeling of disciplining hearing and body to conform to patterns is curiously satisfying. Watching "Trooping the Colour" on Horse Guards Parade has an excitement about it and has meaning. It expresses poetry in motion — almost a form of ballet.

It demonstrates a disciplining of mind not to be sneezed at. The Guards regiments are the supreme example of this. One remembers that at Dunkirk the Guards formed a protective rim half way round the port, to protect other sections of service personnel during the hours they took to embark. The Guards did not retreat and very many died in their positions.

Towards the end of my period at Greenford the pressure eased off a bit. Some of the radar girls, including me, were roped in for a review with chorus, planned by some of the civilians at the depot. We learned to tap dance. I can still do it. We learned to high-kick with linked arms. I was good, too! I can't do that now! Before we could get up to Cochrane standards, we were posted to workshops — 22nd Coy REME Upton Cheshire.

CHAPTER
FOUR

Work as a Mechanic

When I heard that we were being posted to Upton, I was amused and intrigued as memories came flooding in: for Liverpool was my home city and I must digress a little. Upton was on the Wirral and only a few miles from Heswall which had been my home. Before the war our family used to take the car into Birkenhead, on our way into Liverpool. In my childhood, we took the car on special ferry-boats and parked in Lime Street railway station. Later we drove through the new Mersey Tunnel, opened in 1934. In the early months of the war I had decided not to take up my university place at Oxford, but to join one of the services. I needed a secretarial training for that, so my parents arranged for me to attend Miss Foster's Secretarial College in the Cunard Building — or was it the Liver Building? The college was on the Liverpool waterfront and the way to get there was on the ferry-boat from Birkenhead. The Royal Daffodil and the Iris alternated with each other crossing and re-crossing the Mersey all through the day. This route was part of the King's Highway and therefore could never be discontinued, so the ferries sailed even in the thickest fogs. Huge bells rang in

Birkenhead and Liverpool on the dockside so that the captains did not lose direction in bad visibility and everywhere there were foghorns sounding their mournful notes.

I loved the ferry-boats. They had two decks and in the better weather one could walk round and round on the top deck, looking at the shipping. Otherwise one stayed on the lower deck, sitting on wooden slatted seats, gazing out at the water with feet dangling over the vents through which, if one lowered one's head, one could see the Lascars tending the engines, while a blessed draught of warm air came up from the engine room to warm one's legs. There was also a very distinctive smell of warm fuel — coke or oil, dust and sweat — I do not know but I can still smell it. On the top deck one could see across the width of the Mersey to the waterfront of this great wealthy city. There were many docks, cranes, liners sailing to India and other parts of the world, an over-head railway, small steamers and large steamers, tenders and yachts and tug-boats and pilots' boats and dredgers. In the early days of the war it was fascinating to be able to identify where many of the ships came from. Ships from so-called "neutral" countries had to identify themselves, so that the Germans would not bomb them. They carried huge hoardings on deck with the flags or colours of their country. So one could say to oneself, "That's a Norwegian one" or "That's a Dutch one". When I was crossing each day, to get to my course, it was still the period of the "phoney war" so the real war had not yet disrupted all that activity surrounding the busy port.

When France fell, we came out in the lunch hour to see the posters. Then began a few weeks of intense activity. The streets were full of officers and other ranks from the foreign services of several countries. There were French sailors with red pom-poms on their berets. There were Polish troops and there were French officers looking very romantic with their colourful round hats and swirling cloaks. Many ships had brought them in and who sorted them out I do not know: but after a few days they vanished like the wind. Many of the French had the opportunity to return to their home country and did so. Some, of course, stayed and eventually joined De Gaulle.

Liverpool has always had a great deal of meaning for me. My mother spent some of her childhood there. My grandmother had died when I was about 12, so my mother sold the Liverpool properties which she had inherited. It was lucky as they would most likely have been obliterated during the raids on Liverpool, whose destruction was pretty appalling. The Inksters had many associations with the city. My father was a banker there. My father's father was the captain of a sailing ship, the Hellens, a barque, registered in Liverpool. My father and his brothers and sisters were brought up in Aberdeen and attended Aberdeen University. My father, however, was born in the China Seas, as Isabella, his mother, sailed with her husband, in quite comfortable captain's quarters. I have a ship's portrait of the Hellens in my dining room.

Our posting to Upton in Cheshire to the 22nd Workshop Company was our introduction to work on the anti-aircraft sites in Lancashire, Cheshire and North Wales. It must have seemed to the male staff like an enormous invasion, as the ATS postings nearly doubled the number of mechanics working from Upton. We were not spoilt or sheltered from what was quite a tough working life. When a party of four or five people was sent out on a job, it would consist of two or three girls and two men or any variation on the mixture. We were expected to carry equipment, work on the aerials, twenty feet up, spend an hour or two on the roof in rain and wind or do anything the men would do and we were very happy to do that.

One of our regular tasks was very popular. It was to service the radar on the good ship Coronation. We all liked that particular day out for two main reasons. The Coronation was a converted dredger which sailed out onto the outskirts of Liverpool Bay, with radar on board. About once a month she came into Liverpool to dock for servicing. We radar mechanics enjoyed the novelty of going on board and having a breath of sea air. We liked, meeting the crew and being a little bit spoilt by them. We liked most of all, coming home to Upton with huge slabs of naval chocolate, even though they were rock-hard and had to be broken up with a hammer.

There was also another trip which I never had the luck to embark on. There were floating forts — the Maunsel forts — at the edge of Liverpool Bay. One of my staff sergeant friends used to go out to them and described long gangways over the waves. I knew about them to my cost, as I had entrusted a good gold wristwatch to him to mend and he came back very crestfallen, to confess that he had it in a bag which dropped into the sea, when he was going from one fort to another. A story I had to believe for what it was worth.

To return to the Coronation. A party of us went out on a day trip to the dock where she lay. There were five of us, two men and two girls plus a driver. A delightful corporal Bill was in charge. He must have been regarded as responsible, able to keep an eye on the two ATS girl mechanics! I regarded him as "middle aged". He must have been about thirty. He had sight in only one eye because of an accident on his radar training course at Gainsborough. Bill had been out one evening and when he got to the camp gate on his return he was challenged by an inexperienced man on guard duty. "Halt. Who goes there?" Bill gave his name. "Advance and be recognised." Bill advanced right onto the point of the sentry's bayonet. He was lucky not to be killed, but he lost an eye. Such a misfortune could not have happened to a nicer man.

When we got on board The Coronation, the first thing I remember was having to climb down a vertical twenty foot ladder into the hold. I did not like that much. Much preferred climbing up aerials to climbing down into a rather dark hold. The Lister generator for the radar was down there. I honestly did not know much about generators, so I imagine I must have been going down just to get it started.

When we had finished all the repairs and modifications to the equipment, we were invited into the petty-officers' mess for a light meal and drinks. I think they were determined to get the girls tight. The drinks came quickly, one after the other. We were good little girls on the whole and not heavy drinkers. We were determined not to get drunk and let the side down. Both of us ended up by passing our drinks surreptitiously to Bill. He held up remarkably well until we were on shore and in the truck ready to go home when he burst into drunken song. The other REME craftsman knew that Bill had made arrangements to go on leave that evening and knew Bill's home address in Liverpool, so that was where we took him, singing his heart out. We drew up at his garden gate and the driver and craftsman supported him up quite a long garden path. He shouted repeatedly, "The things I do for England!" He was met at his front door by a decidedly wrathful-looking wife. Bill's escort explained to her what had happened to make him drink so much and Bill told us when he got back from leave that his wife had seen the funny side of it and had forgiven him.

Some of the radar research we were involved in was quite good fun, though physically demanding. There was a small team of us, two ATS and two men, with a corporal in charge. The powers-that-be wanted to experiment with the working of Mark II in different settings. We took a receiver and transmitter (the same one each time) to three or four different placements, set it up and dismantled everything the following day. Obviously someone knowledgeable must have done some complicated testing after we had set up the radar equipment in its various locations. My memory remains a complete blank about this. All I know is that these days of research helped in some more generalised research, resulting in the introduction of the GL Mat — of which more later. As we went from place to place with an armed guard we thought we were the cat's whiskers. One setting we went to was amidst rolling hills. One was by the sea — almost on the beach. One was on a twenty-foot ramp in an all-male gun site. This last was the most trying for us girls, because the Battery Commander was such an old woman. We mechanics had been rushing up and down the ramp all day with dipoles and other bits and pieces clutched in our arms and then climbing another twenty feet to the top of the aerial ladder. When the CO arrived we were astounded to see him coming up the ramp on his hands and knees. He obviously hated the idea of two women on his site and made life as difficult as possible for us. There were no "ladies" loos and although some simple precautions could have meant this was no problem, he made it one. He would not have the girls sleeping anywhere in the quarters, although there was a medical sickbay: so we were told we had to sleep in the radar transmitter. We were given a rug each and I slept curled round the TX steering column. It was alright while the Lister generator was still running, but after if was turned off for the night it was beastly cold.

We were both so stiff next morning — and unwashed. We could hardly get up and down the ramp. Assembling and dismantling the aerials and ladder and other parts of the equipment took a considerable amount of time.

The RX and TX (receiver and transmitter) of course had to be on wheels in order to be moved. When the wheels were removed the four metal supports had to be adjusted on screws until the cabins were completely level. There was a spirit level in the floor to ensure absolute accuracy. Getting the cabin right could be a fiddly and irritating job. Some pieces of equipment in the set had to be fastened down for moving from place to place. Other sections had to be disconnected. The grids of the very large VT98 transmitter valves had to be disconnected for travelling. Knowing these routines helped me once to come to the aid of a fellow radar maintenance officer when I was commissioned in 1943. He had just received a new transmitter on his gun site. I happened to call in to his site to lend him something. He was scratching his head because he had just switched on and the equipment was not functioning properly. I said, "Have you reconnected the grids?" He hastily disconnected the voltage on the valves and had a look. Sure enough the grids were disconnected. It was something you learned as a mechanic, but not on the officers' course at Petersham.

Talking of disconnecting things — one man's failure to reconnect properly nearly cost me an eye and might have cost me my life. Our team of mechanics were setting up a new receiver and because we were short of time we borrowed two Royal Artillery men to help. They were supposed to have tightened bolts holding very heavy wooden wings on each side of the cabin. On them were mounted some of the aerials. These were dipoles. To cut a long story short they were a bit like large curtain rods. The wing was supposed to have been secured and the fitter had gone off to tea. I was standing underneath. The other gunner got back onto the wing and suddenly it gave way, precipitating man, wing and dipoles onto me. The man's boot hit me in the face, the end of one dipole sliced down between my eyes and there was blood everywhere. By a sheer miracle it did not go through my eye. They hauled me off to the sick room and I think a medical officer appeared. He stemmed the bleeding and patched me up but did not stitch the wound. It was too late to do it next morning when our MO looked at me, by which time my face was an interesting study in scarlet, black and blue. The mark of the aerial is with me to this day and looks like a one sided frown. In my A.B. 64 a Distinguishing Mark is described as "scar on right eyebrow". I am otherwise quite undistinguished!!

Another episode there was — the slip-ring repair. I had just come into the workshop with my tool kit, at about four o'clock one afternoon, having been working all day. One of the male corporals came up and said, "There is an urgent call from a site on the Liverpool side" — (probably the gun site next to Speke Airport). "I found Josie to join us and we need another strong man to make four." I think we had a bite to eat before we set off.

There was a well, set in the floor of the receiver cabin on the Mark II. It housed a set of slip-rings — perhaps twenty of them — which were connected to the cables going to the command post, so that as the cabin rotated there was still contact with information from the radar to the predictors. A naughty little ATS radar operator had spilt a mug full of milky cocoa down the well, shorting out all the slip-rings. We knew it would be a long job, so when we reached the site, it was agreed we should each go off in turn to get supper. We knew, also, why the corporal in charge of our party had to be tall and strong; because the set of slip-rings had to come out and they had to come out from underneath the cabin! They were extremely heavy.

The other male mechanic went off for a meal, then I went, then Josie the other girl and lastly Dick the corporal. By that time Dick had taken the slip-rings out and had taken them to the command post where we were going to work. In the meantime, Josie, bless her heart, had fallen into a pond in the dark. There were occasional hazards like that on some gun sites. Jo was soaked from the waist down, so had to be sent to ATS quarters to be dried out; so there were only three of us for a while to carry on with the job.

It is difficult to describe, but it was a case of stripping each slip-ring off the pile, cleaning it and the piano-wires which went round it and resoldering each connection. We used carbon-tetrachloride in fire extinguishers for the cleaning. It was quite warm and cosy in the command post and we settled down happily for a long session.

After a while, the male mechanic got up and went outside. He came back fairly quickly, but said he had been sick. He wanted to carry on with the job. Shortly afterwards each of us in turn went outside to be sick and then came back to work. We agreed that there must have been something wrong with the supper we had had on the gun site. We gently cursed the cook, but Jo who came later did not seem to be suffering so badly. The gripes in the stomach and a really thudding headache made it difficult to work: but the job had to be finished, so we plodded on, rubbing each cocoa covered brass ring with carbon-tetrachloride until it was spotless and then getting busy on the joints with our soldering irons. It got very hot in there and we all felt worse every minute. We could not understand why we felt so much better as soon as we finished that part of the job, were out of the command post and back to the radar receiver. Funny sort of food poisoning that was. We felt so much better, we thought that before we went on to the next stage, we needed some breakfast. After that, poor Dick had to get under the cabin again and lift the set of slip-rings up into the well, so that we could secure them. By that time, he had strained his chest and had to rest. The remainder of us had to finish the job, which consisted of lying on the floor and reaching down into the well, to fasten in turn about twenty tiny connections, each one carefully numbered. The light from the inspection lamp only just illuminated the numbers, so it was a very slow, painful and precarious process. It was lunchtime before we finished.

By two o'clock it was all done and needed to be checked by the Royal Artillery people to make sure they were happy about it. By three o'clock we were away. By four o'clock we were home in Upton, twenty four hours after we left. I had never worked for thirty one hours at a stretch before, in my life. Curiously enough I did not feel sleepy. I felt DRUNK! As I got ready for bed I was decidedly giggly. I slept until lunchtime the following day.

When we turned up at the radar workshop that afternoon, we got a solemn talking-to. Captain John Balmer, our CO had us in his office. "A good job done" — But did we realise how dangerously we had behaved? Apparently there was nothing wrong with the supper on the gun site. The carbon-tetrachloride, combined with the heat from the soldering irons, had been producing a deadly gas in a very confined space. Possibly, if we hadn't each had to go outside into the fresh air to be sick from time to time, opening and shutting the door, we might all have succumbed to the gas and that would have been that for our little group.

That was not the only "ticking off" that I got. There was one other. One of the modifications which had to be made to all Mark II sets involved taking the back off a main wooden cabin of the receiver. We had a long pole with which to lever the back away from the roof — something we never normally had to do. We were an all-girl team of three that day and all went well until we came to replace the door. We were not quite strong enough to do it. After a heave and a struggle, it was almost in place, but we had to give it a final bash with a hammer. We heaved sighs of relief and took ourselves home.

Next day came retribution! John Balmer summoned me to his office. A complaint had been made by the Battery Commander of that site. We had dared to chip paint off the top of the door of his precious radar receiver! I said lamely, "Only a little," but batteries took great pride in their equipment and I was hauled over the coals for the damage we had caused. I should have got help from the Royal Artillery which I was too proud to do. The odd reprimand never did a young person any harm.

The thing I remember most about Upton is the kindness and helpfulness of all the men who were already there, from the Captain John Balmer, downwards through senior NCOs to corporals. They treated us as valuable people who had come to do a job. They treated us much better than any of the ATS NCOs or officers had treated us, except for those in my beloved 476 Battery in Hampstead later on.

In mid 1942, Royal Electrical and Mechanical Engineers, REME came into being. We had been anticipating it for some time and we were all delighted. New badges with an electrical flash on them were issued to all radar mechanics and we proudly sewed them on to our sleeves. At about the same time, the girls in the Mixed Heavy AA Batteries were proudly starting to wear the white lanyards of the Royal Artillery.

One thing we were very meticulous about (apart from the momentary lapses into laziness of late adolescence) was the cleanliness of our tools and tool-boxes. Inevitably when mechanics were working out of doors, spanners and files got wet and if left would rust. When back in workshops, everything had to be dried off, cleaned and, if it was appropriate, oiled.

Circuits and electrical parts required high standards of cleanliness, so the benches on which we worked had to be clean. Everything had to be almost as hygienic as an operating theatre. We could have taught modern hospital cleaners a thing or two.

I remember particularly the company sergeant-major, an Aberdonian. He had the blackest hair I have ever seen, short cropped. He took us under his wing from the start, at work and at play. He arranged dances for us. He even took a party of six of us to the sea-side one day! He cast a fatherly eye over us.

At one dance I remember with glee, we were lectured by a short-legged "elderly" sergeant from the main REME workshop (not radar). He told us he was an ex-clown. With an amused eye he watched one of the girls following a good-looking officer with her eyes. He grinned at us and said pointedly, "It's no good pursuing *him*." The officer was what we used to call a queer, though it wasn't apparent.

Later, having studied us "professionally" in a considering sort of way he said: "You girls want to make the most of yourselves. You need to do *this*." I can still see this funny-looking little man solemnly licking a finger, running it along under his lower eyelids and curling his eyelashes! They all looked after us in their own way.

I mentioned that I was ambidextrous. That did not prevent my hands and nails from becoming quite scarred and calloused. A soldering-iron which slipped would cause nasty blisters and these seemed to proliferate. A file would take the surface off the skin of our hands. A stubborn screw or bolt could chip nails or break them. I had taken great care of my hands and nails before the war. Somehow I got out of the habit. I was amused to hear Molly Rose who flew in Air Transport Auxiliary throughout the war complain about what her engineering work did to her hands and I sympathise.

Another sad recollection was of army tea. When radar mechanics were working on a set during the night, the kind kitchen orderlies on the RA gun site would send over a bucket of tea for us. It was almost invariably a bright orange in colour and thick. We dipped our mugs into it when we got desperate.

There was, however, one difficulty we experienced. The ATS top brass did not seem to have realised what ATS radar-mechanics would be doing. Whereas ATS girls working with the Royal Artillery as plotters or radar operators were issued with full battledress, boots, gaiters and hand muffs, we poor mechanics were not. All we had were dungarees. In summer it was all right, but in winter, "Oh boy, were we cold!" When you are up an aerial ladder twenty feet from the ground, there is little protection from the weather and the aerials were a major source of trouble in the Mark 2 radar equipment. We piled on sweaters and warm pants under our denims but they did not solve the problem. Eventually the inevitable happened. I had been out on a gun site in the snow. I think we were fitting the new IFF equipment and that meant new additional aerials on the roof of the cabin. Next morning I could not get out of bed and had the ignominy of being carted off to a camp reception station on a stretcher. I had what used to be called lumbago and badly infected kidneys and was in the CRS for three weeks.

At Upton we did have a slightly more relaxed regime than we had at Greenford and had time for occasional dancing or parties. We also put on one or two plays. One comedy chosen had a title with "Paradise" in it (not "Laughter in Paradise"). My father used to take the family to the theatre in Liverpool before the war. The Liverpool Playhouse had a reputation for very good drama — frequently plays which were afterwards to go to West End theatre in London. I remembered seeing this play with the family.

The gist of the story of the comedy was that of a seventeen-year-old girl who fell in love with a most unsuitable older boyfriend. She was a highly excitable romantic little thing, an ingénue who was carried away by her boyfriend's theories. I think they were theories about nature: not nudism but the importance of things in the natural world. Everything had to be natural — more natural than nature. Strangely enough I remember almost nothing about the dialogue or the plot, although I enjoyed the experience of acting so much. I let myself go and over-acted appallingly. The thing that made me lose my inhibitions was the personality of my suitor. We had searched hard to find a man willing to take this unattractive part. We found one: a great sport. He was a REME NCO — staff sergeant de Paris. He was very tall indeed — tall and gangly. His build was like that of someone who had suffered from overproduction of growth hormone and his face conformed to pattern. He was very popular in the Workshop and one of the nicest people there, with a great sense of humour about himself. He was no romantic figure! In his romantic role he quickly acquired a nickname — that of one of the cheaper scents on the market — Soir de Paris. We had a lot of fun and the production was received with much hilarity.

I never had another leading part in a play again. The agonies of stage fright before the performance were too much for me and made a coward of me, even though I thoroughly enjoyed being on the stage once we had started. One thing I liked enormously about the performance was wearing a very pretty Liberty cotton dress. It was the only garment that had survived the bombing of my home. After wearing uniform day in and day out, the feeling of unrestricted freedom and lightness was intoxicating.

I think I was a corporal at that time and one of the more senior NCOs among the girls. It just happened that the powers-that-be were considering training ATS as radio maintenance officers. Anyway, somehow or other, I was due to go and be interviewed by the local ATS Senior Commander (equivalent to a Major) about the possibility of OCTU training. My dear and very determined father knew that we had been complaining for some time about inadequate clothing. He insisted that when I went for interview I should threaten to write to my member of parliament if I did not get a promise of instant action on our battledress boots and so on. In fact the Senior Commander turned out to be most concerned and we got all we needed within a week.

CHAPTER
FIVE

OCTU (Officer Cadet Training Unit)

In early summer of 1943, I was summoned to an ATS OCTU Board in Hampstead. The previous night was spent in a bed-sitter in a block of flats in Oxford Street, where Bourne and Hollingsworth staff were normally housed. I went by underground to Hampstead and walked up a steep hill (Holly Hill?) to a very large Victorian house, where candidates spent two or three days. Life was made as comfortable for us as could be in wartime conditions. The food was good and there were no obvious signs of us being vetted for table manners and being turned down because we used the wrong spoon or fork.

One of the things I remember puzzled and intrigued me at the time. Throughout the ground floor there were several small tables with jigsaw puzzles on them. I still wonder about the purpose of these. Were they to attract people who wanted an escape from social contacts around them? Were they to indicate obsessional traits? Were they to demonstrate mathematical or special skills? Were they quite innocently there to give people a short respite from the stresses of the weekend? Whatever their purpose, I was a bit cagey about being seen wrestling with the pieces and kept well clear of them. So they did not find out anything about *me* from the jigsaws.

We underwent a series of tests which were new to me, but have since become commonplace. One was the Rorshach test in which one was required to state what a series of inkblots called to one's mind. There was a word-association test in which a number of single words were flashed onto a screen and we were given only a second or two to write down a response — no time to dwell on what might be the most impressive answer. This test seemed to be of importance to the examiners, because some candidates were singled out after it to meet a psychiatrist. My answers appeared not to be interesting or sinister enough to merit an interview.

In another session we were taken out on to a lawn in groups of ten and lined up single file, facing up the lawn. We were told that a plane would be flying over and we were required to use our nine fellow members to form a code letter on the ground. This might have been easy, but all instructions about where to place themselves had to be given before anyone moved. So, for instance, if the letter was R you had to get the ones on the left finally in a straight line, the middle lot in a curve and the right hand ones in a slant. Each had to take a different number of steps forward and to one side or the other. You said "start" and then "halt" and "lie down". If your calculations were right, you hoped people would do as instructed. Most people managed fairly well, but some instructions got a bit incoherent.

In a different outdoor exercise, one volunteer was strapped to a stretcher and the other nine had to manoeuvre the stretcher through a series of hazards. In one place we had to get the volunteer over a really high wall. At one point I remember vividly she was hanging head downwards, almost completely vertical, while the other participants struggled on the far side of the wall. The stretcher-case certainly merited points for bravery.

The most hilarious test of the whole weekend took place indoors. Ten of us were ushered into a large room with a thick carpeting of straw. Down one side of the room was a sort of corridor, cut off from the rest of the space by chicken wire. In this space, observing us, were about eight senior officers — several being staff officers. We were told that as a party we had become lost on a moor in the snow and had come across this hut where we would have to take shelter for the night. We would find objects to help us under the straw. We all started looking under the straw and found firewood, boxes of matches, cans of water, blankets, tins of biscuits, etc. etc. Now came the amusing part. The brass hats were obviously wanting to find out something about us individually. We had each to act out a part, to demonstrate certain qualities we thought the authorities would be looking for.

It was important to show that we functioned well as members of a group and knew how to cooperate: that we could adopt out appropriate role within the group. Equally important, however, was that we should demonstrate leadership talent, the so-called "officer qualities". The result was that the really bossy applicants started shouting, "Do this. Do that." Those of us who were not naturally so aggressive, but wanted to show that we knew what was what, started saying, "Come on, folks, we've to get the place clean and dry." The shyer, less confident people waited to be told what to do. Some of us alternated between groups one and two and conflicting ideas made life very difficult. The results for the lookers on must have been very funny.

After two or three days of trying to show good points and conceal bad points in my personality, I felt pretty exhausted and retreated to Upon without any idea how I had got on.

The run up to OCTU was a series of disasters. I think if I had not been up for a technical commission in radar, I might have been thrown out in the early days.

After the OCTU Board I knew I was accepted for training in Windsor. I did not hear from them and did not hear from them. I was overdue for leave so asked Mary Woolvern, my little ATS officer, if I could take a week's leave and go to see my parents in Oxford. She thought it a good idea, so I got myself to Lime Street Station in Liverpool with my suitcase to catch a train to Oxford. I put the case on a rack in a compartment and got out again to get a magazine from the bookstall. While I was on the platform I heard an announcement over the Tannoy: "Will Corporal Inkster please telephone her company officer." Well, there just was no time, was there! Could not get my luggage off the train! So I leapt into the compartment and off I went.

When I arrived at my parents' hotel in Oxford, my mother said, "Darling, there's a telegram for you from Upton." To my horror it said "Report to OCTU Windsor on Thursday", which was the following day. After an evening meal I caught a train back to Liverpool, arriving late at night. There was no way I could get out to Upton until early morning. The Services in their wisdom had provision for poor souls like me who were stranded in Lime Street Station. We slept on rather hard mattresses on the floor of the waiting room with minimal covering over us — about ten stranded service girls. Someone woke me for my early train to Upton.

Back at my billet, life was hell. I had to pack up everything in about two hours. Mary Woolvern gave me my instructions for the journey from Liverpool to Windsor, carefully contrived for me by a benevolent Railway Transport Office. I had four changes on the way. I was like a snail carrying everything on my back with five items of luggage, one being a heavy kit bag. I do remember vividly that, at two of the stations en route, I had to get all my possessions across a bridge over a railway-line. Needless to say, I arrived at OCTU almost in a state of collapse. My very pleasant squadron officer told me a fortnight later that in the first few days she had seriously considered whether I was fit "officer material". Luckily I was able to bounce back and cope with the course.

BORING. Oh how boring it was! How does one describe a boring experience without being boring about it?

Of course, some of the trouble arose from the fact that I was dying to get on with my technical radar training at Petersham. The lectures and discussions at Windsor seemed so irrelevant to my future job, though I cannot have known then that I would be in charge of men not girls. At OCTU there was a curious attitude to "other ranks", as if they were inferior beings and had to be treated in a certain way: whereas both in the FANY and as a radar mechanic my experience had been of being treated with respect, as a contributing member of a team.

At Windsor we rehearsed endlessly situations in which other ranks had been AWOL (absent without leave) or had committed more minor misdemeanours, such as being late or failing to read and obey orders. We learnt how to compose Part I and Part II Orders. I will not trouble you with explanations of what those were, but I never had to compose another after leaving OCTU. Each of us was required to deliver lecturettes to our particular group of about 20 cadets. Most were excruciatingly dull, but we did have Barbara Bairnsfather in our team. She was the daughter of Bruce Bairnsfather the famous cartoonist of the First World War. He depicted scenes showing the humour of the troops in places of fear and tragedy. One cartoon was of two privates in a shell hole. "If you knows a better 'ole, go to it!" Barbara had inherited much of his humour and made us laugh. I tried to relieve the tedium by giving instruction on soldering a joint in which my tie fell forward and got burnt on the soldering iron. It had once happened to me.

So little else I remember about what we learnt. The only real experience was being duty cadet one night. I had to sleep on the floor in the Duty Room, with instructions about what to do in case of amber and red alerts. Amber meant I had to get up and put battle dress and shoes on in pitch darkness. When, to my surprise I got a "Red Alert", I had to rouse the whole OCTU (before the air raid warning sounded outside). We all had to trudge down to the air raid shelters underground and I had to do my share of checking that no-one was missing. For once, I actually felt I had some real responsibility and knew I enjoyed it.

There were 200 cadets at Windsor and the authorities may have deliberately separated the REME cadets. We were pretty naughty at OCTU because we believed we could not be turned down for a commission, having been selected for a technical one. I never encountered the other two and indeed never knew they were there. If I had, we might have had a giggle together. I remember being rather lonely at times. This was the one time in my life when I failed to find congenial company. Luckily it was only for three months and perhaps one learns something extra about oneself through an experience like that.

Two highlights relieved the monotony. One was a visit from Joyce Grenfell who came to speak at a Guest Night dinner. She was brilliant. The other was another Guest Night visitor — the admiral who as a child was the original of "Bubbles" and turned out to be very good fun.

My other interesting recollection was of a parade of cadets through Windsor in War Weapons Week. We marched through the central courtyard of the Castle, with an "Eyes right" to the figures on a dais. The King and Queen were there and the two Princesses — Elizabeth being still in her midteens and very young looking. Towering over them all was the figure of King Haakon of Norway, a tall man indeed. I still have a photograph of the parade in the courtyard.

Princess Elizabeth was very enthusiastic about doing her bit and at the age of 18 managed to get herself into uniform and trained as a driver and mechanic in the ATS — trained by drivers from the First Aid Nursing Yeomanry.

Route marches were part of the OCTU training and the weather was very hot. Marches therefore meant over-heated bodies and blistered feet. What one longed for, on return to base, was a nice soak in a really hot bath. Of course, baths were restricted to a depth of five inches of water, but one could normally lie flat in that, even if it did not cover one's tummy. But could this be enjoyed at OCTU? No, it could not.

The first time I got the chance to besport myself in one of the bathrooms I got a rude shock. I was confronted with a sight I had never seen before and — thank God — have never seen since; a SITZBATH. A sitzbath was roughly the shape of a bath-chair, without wheels of course and in porcelain. One sat on the upper section and put one's feet in the well. It was impossible to relax: I suppose one was not meant to in a sitzbath. One's bottom was on the cold porcelain seat while one's feet were in a warm trough. In a normal bath, the whole of the bottom of the bath is warmed by the water. By the time you swilled the warm water over your shoulders, it was cold. The whole experience was diabolic.

At the end of our course we received our first payment as officers in cash. It was in the form of an old type £5 note. Few but the elderly will remember seeing one of these. The note was twice the size of a modern bank note. It was pure white, of very thin material, very tough, difficult to crush. It was much more valuable than its modern equivalent and often had several signatures on it — those of people through whose hands it had passed. Unfortunately mine soon got spent.

CHAPTER
SIX

Petersham Course

Before going to OCTU (Officer Cadet Training Unit) in 1943 I was interviewed by a REME captain, to ascertain whether I was competent enough to undertake the officers' technical training at Petersham. He asked me some questions which I thought were rather difficult and because I was nervous I do not think my answers were brilliant.

Anyway, at the end of the interview, he said resignedly: "Well, you'll be doing the Petersham course before you are let loose on an unsuspecting world." So, after a thoroughly boring OCTU course at Windsor, to Petersham I went.

Someone had warned me that some knowledge of calculus would be of advantage on the Petersham course. After all, they had a reputation to keep up. I therefore bought myself a little green book on the subject. It looked as though it might be able to convey some useful thoughts to people of my low grade intelligence. On the fly-leaf it said: "What one fool can do, any fool can do." However, after struggling with the text for a bit, I decided that I belonged to a different category of fools. I spent some time in lectures diligently copying down into my note book strings of formulae — Delta this over Delta that, which conveyed to me only a modicum of meaning. I am no mathematician and could never say

"I am very good at integral and differential calculus.
I am the very model of a modern Major-General."
(Pirates of Penzance)

It was very reassuring to discover that only a very few officers on our course could follow all the mathematics with ease. We learnt about phasing on the aerial system and I think I really understood a little more than was essential in an RMO's job. After all, we were not going to have to change the wavelengths on our sets every day: nor were we going to be required to do advanced research. We did need to understand the workings of all the various circuits in our equipment and diagnose faults caused by malfunctioning valves, condensers, resistors, aerials and motors.

Some things my memory refuses to recall. Did we take lectures and practical work on both gun-laying radar and searchlight radar (which was called Elsie) at the same time? I think we must have done, because the examinations for these two spheres of work alternated, one week an exam concerned with searchlight radar and the next week one on gun-laying. We certainly learned about both and the first examination to come up was a searchlight one. I remember almost nothing about the searchlight equipment, because I never worked on it. I vaguely recall learning about sound-locators which, incidentally, the Germans were using at this time. If one was off target, the impulses coming from the plane one was trying to follow reached each ear of the operator at different times, in different phases. The equipment was turned until the operator was facing the target directly. Operators had to be selected carefully, however, because some people thought they were spot-on when they were not. They had what we were intrigued to hear was called Binaural Squint!! My mind was set on working with gun-laying radar. I did something quite naughty: I sat through an exam with five questions of searchlight radar and wrote only two answers. You had to obtain at least 50% marks, so I *had* to fail. The following week I took and passed an exam on gun-laying equipment.

After all it did make sense. I had worked for two years on GL Mark II, had delved into its innards, done modifications on it and had opportunities to pick the brains of our splendid staff-sergeants at Upton. I found the searchlight radar boring. Anyway, I suspect I wanted to be involved in the gun sites in retaliation for what the German bombers had done to my home. At the end of the course I passed out satisfactorily: though what J. A. Ratcliffe, founder of the Petersham Course, with his high standards of academic knowledge would have made of the motley crew in our group Heaven only knows! One or two of the men were very experienced in radio theory and went on to higher things.

Some memories of Petersham have become rather hazy. I remember a rather attractive building, which I think was the original rectory, damaged by a plane during my course. There was another building which probably had been a church hall. Additionally, there were Nissen huts dotted about among trees. As we were there in summer there were none of the agonies of cold and wet which our class had suffered at Gainsborough in January 1942.

Many happenings which stand out in one's memory are tragi-comic. During an afternoon's tuition at Petersham, my group of students was in a Nissen hut quite near the School. A parallel group was having an exhibition of how to calibrate the radar equipment. This was performed in the open air. A plane from Croydon airfield was instructed to fly round and round at various heights, so that the accuracy of the equipment could be checked. This was, as you can imagine, an extremely boring way of spending the afternoon for the pilot and wireless operator. Frequently the air crew were "naughty boys" who had committed some minor misdemeanour or had annoyed a senior officer in some way.

In this case, the calibration lesson had been completed and a "home to tea" message was sent to the Anson Trainer. The rather bolshy pilot decided to celebrate with a victory roll: but you cannot do a victory roll safely in an Anson. The first thing we heard in our Nissen hut was a peculiar sort of screaming noise, a swish and a thud. When we rushed outside, pieces of yellow canvas were floating through the air. The plane had disintegrated and the engine and fuselage had crashed into the back of the radar school, carrying the two crew members with it.

As we rushed towards the school, to see what we could do to help, we ran into a thick haze of petrol vapour and hastily extinguished all cigarettes. I looked up at the wall facing us and two sensations struck me instantaneously. One was realisation that the RAF men and possibly people in the school must have died. The other was an appreciation of a fantastically comic scene of people at every window in the place, all looking out with various expressions on their faces. All were as white as millers, not with fear but with plaster from the ceilings, shaken by the impact of the crash. The tragicomedy of the situation has remained with me until now.

There was more to follow. The plane had crashed at an angle, into the part of the building where the commandant's office was. Above the office was a lecture room in which about 20 trainee radar officers had been about 10 minutes before. Everyone started saying, "How awful! The Headmaster must be in the wreckage." If he had been, he could not have survived. People said, "What a tragic loss of a distinguished scientist." While search of the rubble was going on half an hour later, the Headmaster — probably Dr J. A. Harrison — came rather shamefacedly up the drive. He had sneaked off to the cinema that afternoon without telling anybody. That was the story, anyway!

There was a hall to which we went for our "elevenses" which I think included rather delicious sticky buns. As one entered, one met a cloud — almost a wall — of blue Woodbine smoke. Almost everybody in the place was smoking, including me. We got a weekly allowance of cigarettes, for which we paid a low price. Mainly they were Woodbines, but occasionally there was a packet of Players, Senior Service or another of the better brands. The girls had cigarette cases, holding ten and I remember mine was a very pretty little gold-plated box with an elaborate pattern of coloured flowers on the front. We never gave a thought to the effects of smoking on our lungs and in a way it was a self-defensive exercise. If one smoked, one did not notice the smell of other people's smoke, or the taste of smoker's mouth on one's own!

I acquired one or two boyfriends at Petersham, but there was nothing serious. One was a very good-looking Canadian called Butch. He seemed to appear from nowhere, not on our course and was determined to pursue me. I was attracted to men who did the chasing as I was too shy to do it myself. He was amusing and good company. I was a slow starter and it might have got serious. He had had a fiancée in Canada but there had been a bad quarrel and a complete break. He was not staying in our billet, but we used to sit on the stairs and talk for hours if it was raining or stroll along the riverbank at Richmond on a fine evening. I must have wanted to impress, because I had just received a beautiful silk housecoat, made with material bought in Oxford at Eliston and Cavell (pre-war stock). I was sitting in this robe with the two girls I shared a room with, expecting him to turn up. When he did, it was to tell me that he had received a make-it-up letter from his ex-fiancée and he thought he wanted to renew the engagement. He told me very nicely but I was quite annoyed and I remember throwing a book at him. I was not heartbroken, however, and I felt it was just as well. My sister Brenda, who belonged to a far more conventional set than I, had said that I could not possibly get serious about someone called Butch!

My Canadian boyfriend cheered my spirits at a difficult time. I found radar theory enthralling, but I cannot deny that I found the theory of it all at Petersham level quite hard going and very demanding. We were told that on passing out successfully we had reached degree standard in that branch of physics which related to radar. In 1939 I had not even taken any of the sciences or mathematics at Higher School Certificate level: all my specialist subjects were to do with language.

Another boyfriend after that was a very tall, elegant looking red-head who was staying in our house. We met over the billiard table and walked miles along the river bank. I quickly cooled off, however, because he had a nasty habit of biting my lips when he kissed me: an odd nip would have been acceptable but these were really hard bites which drew blood. I wanted something a bit more romantic, so suggested we parted.

Two or three of us used to go down to the local pub on those glorious summer evenings. Our local was The Lass and it was a while before we realised it was on the wrong Richmond Hill: the song refers to the Richmond Hill in Yorkshire. We sat outside in the sweltering heat. A pony and trap used to draw up very often and the dear little pony, being just as thirsty as we were, enjoyed a pint of beer brought to him by his master.

Our group of trainees was billeted in a very large house on Richmond Hill. It was all rather run down, but clean and warm with adequate food, hot water and spacious bedrooms. It was run by a funny little elderly woman with dyed red hair — dark roots showing. The rumour went round and was believed by us, that pre-war her house had been a brothel.

On subsequent up-dating courses, I had the luck to be billeted with dear Miss Julius and her devoted maid, in a house just down the lane from the School. She was an old aristocrat, but rather impoverished. In her eighties she was still mowing her own lawn and climbing up the side of her house to deal with her espalier pear trees. During one course I shared a bedroom with a WRAF officer, a cousin of Greer Garson, the film star of "Mrs Miniver" and extraordinarily like her. She was married and was able to meet her husband at the weekends. She travelled each day by underground from Richmond to the Air Ministry where she worked.

I stayed with Miss Julius when I was on a course dealing with the Canadian Radar Mark III. It was a disastrous course for me. On the second day I developed bad pains in what turned out to be an impacted wisdom tooth. An appointment was made for me with an army dentist in Richmond. I did not know what was in store for me. The young dentist decided to operate there and then. I had no idea that an impacted wisdom tooth was generally dealt with in hospital. He injected the first batch of pain killer and got to work. After a considerable time of hacking at my jaw, he gave me more pain killer. Much later, he got the tooth out, but had to do some considerable stitching inside my mouth. He took so long to do the operation that one of his colleagues came in to see what was happening. He took one look inside my mouth, said "My God!!" and went out again.

I was delivered back to my billet in Petersham in due course, in rather a shaky state, and after some soup retired to bed. The next day my face had swollen up to enormous proportions and I could only open my mouth about two inches. I was expected to continue with the Canadian Radar course, because I needed the knowledge back at Hampstead. I found it very difficult to take in all the information I was being given. I can still recall the pain and discomfort of my mouth and face. It was impossible to get a toothbrush between my teeth and even to get solid food into my mouth. I existed on soup, fruit purées, jelly, scrambled egg and porridge. Naturally, talking and communicating properly was difficult. I left Petersham with a somewhat vaguer idea of the Canadian equipment than I had hoped.

My jaw remained fixed with minimal opening for several weeks, and eventually it was decided that the young dentist might have broken my jaw and I was referred to the Army Dental Centre in Grays Inn Road. It was no longer very painful, except when I laughed, and I was regarded with some concern and amusement in the officers' mess. People kept offering me large humbug sweets and other things I could not get between my teeth. Eventually the infection died down and I could open my jaw fairly normally, but it took several months to clear properly. However, I had to learn about the new equipment "on the job" and with the help of two newly acquired staff sergeants.

Just before I went on my second Petersham course, on going into Workshops at Park Royal one day, I was informed that I was to get an expanded detachment in the form of two staff sergeants: one for Easy 22 and one for the off-site W14. Their names were, unbelievably, Tinsley and Tansley and in my mind I immediately christened them Tweedle Dum and Tweedle Dee. At first, the only way I could remember which was which was that I put staff sergeant Tansley at Hampstead (there were As in Tansley and Hampstead!).

CHAPTER
SEVEN

My Gun Sites in the Inner Artillery Zone

When I had completed the radar maintenance officer's course I was posted from Petersham. Asked where I wanted to go, I stupidly said "Dorset" where I had friends. As everyone knows, in the Army you never get sent where you ask to go, so I found London on my posting order. It was to be 1st AA Workshop Company. REME, Park Royal. I was the only woman radar officer in London, north of the Thames. I later discovered that there were two in the south based at Kidbrooke Workshops, twin sisters, the Sternes, who had science degrees and were therefore much more highly qualified than I was.

The two REME Workshops at Park Royal Loughton (1st AA Workshop Company) were responsible for the maintenance and repair and accuracy of all radars north of the Thames. There were groups of radar mechanics, craftsmen, corporals, sergeants and staff sergeants, all male on each site. They were attached to the Royal Artillery Mixed Heavy Anti-aircraft Batteries but worked on the sets in a detachment of 5/6 gun sites, under a radar maintenance officer. My detachment consisted of gun sites at Hampstead, Brent, Dollis Hill, Mill Hill, Primrose Hill and Whetstone Park. For a few weeks I looked after the radar at Chequers, an ancient piece of equipment serving the all-male light anti-aircraft regiment guarding the Prime Minister's official home.

I reported to the Major at REME Company Headquarters in the afternoon. He treated me quite normally, but the adjutant, who seemed very elderly to me, treated me in an avuncular way and I almost expected him to pat me on the head. After being put up in a hotel for the night in Golders Green, I was taken in the Major's car to the Workshop at Park Royal and from there, after some formalities, to the Mixed Heavy AA gun site at Hampstead. After leaving Company HQ I was treated like any other officer, much to my relief. I was received very courteously by everyone on 476 battery at Hampstead.

I found at Easy 22 a very friendly and helpful Royal Artillery battery. There was a Battery Commander in his 40s (ex-London Scottish) who was a splendid character with just the right mixture of informality and discipline. There was a Junior Commander (female equivalent of a Captain) who was in charge of all the ATS personnel on the sites, including two or three ATS officers of the mixed battery, but not in charge of me. By the time I arrived on site the ATS officers were taking their turn as Gun Position Officers. The ATS subalterns and I shared a very large attic bedroom and bathroom. Conditions were pretty spartan. There was only one loo for all officers in the Mess. At least we had an officers' mess which was a largish suburban house, across the road from the gun site, rather than the hutted affair of many other gun sites. The site itself was a rather tongue-shaped area at the Golders Green end of Hampstead Heath. This gun site was the one which appeared in a popular film of 1943 "The Gentle Sex". Lesley Howard produced and narrated it. It was the story of a group of ATS recruits and what happened to them in various postings after training. One group was sent to a mixed heavy Ack-Ack gun site (Hampstead) and there were some shots of the girls on the command post with the predictor, during an air raid. Radar was too secret to be shown. All the fun of the shooting of the film happened before I arrived at E22.

From the Officers' Mess one crossed the road to the site and encountered a barrier with a guardroom alongside. There was always a sentry on duty and if one "belonged" to the battery, one just shouted one's name and the bar was lifted. The actual site was quite a large area. It encompassed radar equipment and generators, command post and guns, NAAFI, ATS sleeping quarters and ablutions, men's sleeping quarters, quarter-masters' stores, mess for the troops, sergeants' mess, battery office, REME work hut, my office, generators, garages and emergency water supply tank.

The radar will have most of a chapter to itself later on. The command post was a large concrete area, partly below ground but with a roof or top deck on which rested the various pieces of equipment "manned" by girls trained in predictor work, range, height-finding and so on. Below decks there were several rooms. The plotting room contained a large, squared, transparent screen, illuminated from beneath, which showed the position of planes as they came in. There was room for telephones and intercom and accommodation for the gun position officer. There was some heating in winter and blast curtains over the entrance. There was a chest-high concrete wall round the space on the top deck, giving the girls some protection. This did not save one poor girl at the Hampstead gun site when a piece of shrapnel bounced off this parapet into her eye, blinding her.

The generator shed housed two or three large Lister generators: so the site was not dependent on public supplies. These Listers were remarkably faithful and reliable. They were serviced and repaired from Park Royal Workshop, though my radar staff were capable of a certain amount of first aid. When the Canadian radar came onto Easy 22 in Autumn 1943, it had its own petrol-driven generator.

Next door to the Battery Office was the Nissen hut allocated to the REME. The mechanics worked there doing their soldering, filing, stripping down motors and so on. At one end I had my separate office where I typed my reports, absorbed documents and dealt with quite a lot of reading and written work. I had the great delight of listening to the mechanics' chat which was witty, highly entertaining and enlightening. The Quartermaster had a separate store where one could take items which were designated Beyond Local Repair, in the hope of getting them exchanged. We radar people had to have our own cases of spare valves which were frequently needed.

There were the blocks of huts with sleeping accommodation and the necessary ablutions and messes. The NAAFI was quite large and comfortable and there were regular dances there. ENSA and other concerts happened in the NAAFI and once a memorable, spectacular table tennis exhibition by some national champions. We had numerous dances after which it was a custom to bawl the words of a bawdy song:

"Roll me over, in the clover,

Roll me over, lay me down and do it again!"

The younger girls in their innocence hardly knew what this meant!

A good many of the London gun sites were in public parks. There were at least 69 in the London area, north and south of the Thames. Each had a code name. Hampstead for instance was E22. The site at Dollis Hill was W9. They were always referred to by the names we used on the telephone for alphabet letters. So E22 was Easy-two-two and W14 was Willy-one-four. But then — I nearly forgot — we had Guns! There were three main kinds of guns on the sites — 3.7 inch, 4.5 inch (converted to what they called Mark VI) and 5.25 naval guns. We had a Bofors gun as well. That was quite spectacular during raids as it fired tracers, like a necklace of light in the darkness. A searchlight also arrived at E22 one day — but I think was moved elsewhere quite quickly. The weather was very frosty at the time and when the light was on a beam parallel to the ground, it was delightful to warm oneself in it. There were a number of searchlights in our area and I recall an optical illusion. At night, when the light was extinguished, one seemed to see a black beam against the starry sky.

At Mill Hill (W13) and Primrose Hill (E14) there were the dreaded 5.25 naval guns. These were set in large concrete emplacements and the noise they made was horrific. Colin Dobinson writes: "In truth a battery of four 5.25 anti-aircraft guns was a fearsome thing to put in a city". The noise of the guns when you were actually on the site was almost indescribable.

Security on sites was supposed to be tight, but looking back, I realise there were strange lacunae in it. At the entrance a sentry was on duty day and night: but I have two strange memories. One was of Primrose Hill and one of Dollis Hill. At Primrose Hill I seem to remember that the transmitter cabin for the GL Mark 2 was outside (?) the official gun site, in an allotment! I am almost certain that when I went into the transmitter, which was of course kept locked, there were people digging cabbages round the set! As to the Dollis Hill site, a railway line ran around the northern circumference of the area and was easily accessible over a fence. I go into detail about that elsewhere, with a story about fuel.

We had a large EWS tank on site. Anyone who had anything to do with the town or city during the war would be familiar with those letters, which stood for Emergency Water Supply. Ours was a large, grassy mound with a considerable tank let into it. I am not sure whether this was made of metal or concrete, but its sides were steep and it had a depth of several feet.

One morning I was going across the road from the officers' mess and, as the sentry lifted the barrier for me, I heard a funny sort of yapping noise and a little black and white terrier rushed up to me. There was an unmistakable note of distress in his voice. He was a stranger. Why should he be greeting me like this? I stopped and he looked pleadingly up at me and then dashed across to the EWS tank and up the slope, stopped a minute, then came rushing back to me. Obviously thinking I might not have got the message, he shot back to the tank and stopped, looking pleadingly back at me again.

I followed him and climbed up the slope. A doggie head was bobbing up and down in the water at the side. It belonged to a large retriever who had obviously jumped in and was unable to get out, because the sides of the tank were steep and the water-level was low. Luckily he had a collar. I lay full length on the grassy slope and reached over to get hold of it. He was tiring and his head was half-submerged, but I managed to get his head up high enough for him to breathe properly. More I could not do. There I was, spread eagled on the grass, almost head downwards, hanging on for dear life. Again more I could not do. All I could do was scream blue murder. Luckily it was near the gun-pits and three of the gunners who were working on the guns came rushing over and hauled the heavy, half drowned animal out.

The terrier, his little pal, had saved his life and started dancing round him. After a few minutes recovery time, the two friends trotted off down the road together.

The battery commander, a Major, had charge of E22 and the off site, W9 at Dollis Hill. There was a Captain in residence there. All sorts of amusing things happened at W9. One was the episode with the palings. The captain in charge of W9 decided that the lane leading to the gun site from the main road needed new railings. The lane ran up to the gun site, then past it up to what we were informed was a GPO Research Station. I only discovered in 2002 that the Research Station had beneath it a very important sort of reserve bunker for Churchill and members of the Government.

Gunners were sent to erect a new palisade consisting of sharp-ended stakes hammered well into the ground: and very smart the finished fence looked. The GPO Research Station suffered an inexplicable loss of electrical power which caused some consternation. I think it took a day or two to discover that W9's smart new fence was responsible, because the stakes had severed their mains cable.

There is more of interest in this story. Re-reading recently my book about Bletchley Park "Station X" by Michael Smith, I found a passage about Tommy Flowers and his research on Colossus. Flowers was a very brilliant young engineer who had worked at the GPO Research Station before the war, on the first telephone exchange containing valves instead of old fashioned mechanical relays. A mechanically-based piece of equipment at

Bletchley Park, called Robinson, was giving trouble and Flowers said he could do better with an electronic machine. He reckoned it would take about a year to produce. The code-breakers were sceptical about his idea and thought it would take too long, so he went ahead quietly with designing it at Dollis Hill in February 1943 and made a prototype in 10 months. By 8th December Colossus, as it was called, had been moved to Bletchley Park. Colossus was in fact the first practical application of a large-scale programme-controlled computer and it transformed work at Bletchley Park.

It is awesome to think that our new fence at W9 might have delayed production of Colossus. I think that incident happened early in 1944, by which time Colossus was no longer at Dollis Hill.

CHAPTER
EIGHT

Ack-Ack and Radar

There is a wonderful quotation from Stanley Baldwin, which turned out to be truly wide of the mark. In 1935, speaking of a future possible war, he said: "The bombers will always get through." Maybe it was that fatalistic attitude which caused successive governments to postpone necessary preparations for anti-aircraft services. At the beginning of the war, Hitler prophesied to Unity Mitford that it would take three years for Britain to produce adequate anti-aircraft defences. And so it did. That was one reason why London suffered so badly during the 1940 blitz. Had we had the defences of 1943 in the first blitz, it would have been a totally different story.

The whole purpose of the existence of the gun sites was, of course, to defend London and the rest of the country against enemy bombers. In the early days of the war radar was in its infancy. In 1941–42, the original rather primitive Mark I radar was replaced by the much more sophisticated Mark II on which I mainly worked as a mechanic at Greenford and at Upton, in Cheshire. By the time I was commissioned as a radar maintenance officer in mid-1943 the Canadian

A.A. No. III Mark I was coming into use in the London area and the effectiveness of ack-ack fire was more than doubled.

Frederick Pile, appointed to command the first anti-aircraft division in 1938, was an extraordinarily far-seeing and enlightened soldier. Caroline Hazlett, a noted woman electrical engineer of pre-war days, was consulted about the feasibility of using women on anti-aircraft duties. Discussion took place about the possibility of bringing women in as professionals in technical trades of fire-control and other ancillaries to gunnery. Nothing happened in 1939 and 1940, but early in 1941, two of the worst German raids took place. On April 16th 1941, 712 bombers descended on London and, in mid May, 507 aircraft bombed the city. There was a serious shortage of men in AA units.

The Government was forced into making a new departure. The first mixed anti-aircraft battery was formed in Richmond Park and within two years there were thousands of women working as part of teams in AA batteries. In some ways they were found to be better than the men they replaced. Major Millington in an essay "Women Who Served the Guns" said: "By 1942 there were more women than men in AA Command. The ATS were playing their full part in all the services with Signals, RAC, and REME and Ordnance as well as at Formation Headquarters." I quote this because even Sir Frederick Pile never mentions women working in REME as radar mechanics or radar maintenance officers and Major Millington's comments are the only ones I know. Shelford Bidwell, historian of artillery and of the ATS, wrote: "There is not much essential difference between manning a GL set or a predictor and firing a gun: both are means of destroying enemy aircraft." Sir Frederick Pile, after the war, said: "The girls lived like men, fought their lives like men and, alas, some of them died like men." There were 389 girls in mixed batteries killed or wounded during the war.

At the same time as decisions were made about mixed batteries, decisions must have been made to train women as radar mechanics, so that the first course for us had been planned and organised during the summer. Our course started in September 1941.

Senior ATS officers had a very peculiar attitude to developments in which women were employed in anti-aircraft units. They were very reluctant to co-operate. Perhaps they were afraid that they were going to lose control over the girls. One of the most senior visiting one of the first mixed AA units reminded them, to their dismay, that she could at any time post them away from their batteries to any other units. Whether she could have done so was a moot point. I think Churchill would have had something to say about that.

Certainly the ATS radar mechanics and radar officers felt that the "higher ups in ATS" showed a considerable lack of interest in us. I have described how they failed to arrange for us radar mechanics to be provided with the necessary basic clothing of battle dress, leather jerkins, boots and the rest until a very considerable fuss was made early in 1943. No senior

ATS officer ever came on an official visit to us. We were never kept informed as to which ATS unit we were attached to on paper. All we knew about were our REME postings. A pamphlet issued in 1943, detailing trade tests for all ATS personnel, included the work of radar operators, but never even mentioned radar mechanics, although many by that time had been trained for two years.

Radar is rather technical stuff and I do not know how to describe the equipments without getting into areas which may not be familiar to the general reader: at least to people not acquainted with electronics. It is impossible to go into long explanations about thermionic valves, pulses, grids and wave lengths and such like. You will just have to be patient, let some of it slide over your head and take it as read that bits of the equipment worked and fulfilled the functions they were designed for. Some of the diagrams in this book may help.

The history of the beginning of radar and the story of the people who developed it and those who kept it going is an exciting one. Sir Robert Watson-Watt is generally associated with the beginnings of radar. John Cockcroft, later linked with the flying bedstead, L. H. Bedford of Cossors and B. J. Edwards of Pye were all in with the early research.

In 1937 the first army radio location set, GL Mark I, was introduced. By early 1939, the radar could give the gunners accurate fire control data in range and "creditable" readings in bearing. The sets were built mainly by Cossor. Their range was about 30,000 yards

(17 miles) and fed accurate information on range to the predictor. Bearing information was accurate to 1½ degrees of arc. Elevation was at first a problem, but Mr.Bedford shortly found a solution. I will not go into the technicalities.

Simultaneously, CD/CHL (Coastal Defence/Chain Home Low) was being developed for use on the coast. It gave long-range information, but, once the bombers had passed over, could not be used for gun laying.

A young scientist called Patrick Blackett formed a team of knowledgeable and brilliant scientists working from Horseferry Road in London to service as many of the radar sets as possible on London gun sites. They were an incredible mixture, including a surveyor, one or two biologists and a physiologist from the medical school in Edinburgh. They were christened Blackett's Circus and were responsible for the planning of the Mat for GL Mark II which is described elsewhere.

In October 1940, J. A. Ratcliffe was asked to establish a school for training civilians who already had scientific knowledge, to keep the GL sets in action in the field (ie. on gun sites). The government requisitioned Petersham Hall, near Richmond, where I did my officers' training in 1943. At the end of 1940 it was considered that only people with an established scientific background would be capable of understanding the intricate circuits of the radio location, as it was then called. The first civilian recruits were carefully selected, skilled radio personnel, lent by specialist firms, or schoolmasters of physics and mathematics and even some professors.

By June 1941, Petersham School had trained their first ten or twelve men, all previously experienced in radio or otherwise scientifically qualified. The first batch were sent out to gun sites in the London area, after a course of ten weeks or so. Their function was to keep the radar sets working. They made adjustments, carried out calibration and repaired faults if the RAOC mechanics could not be summoned to the site in time to do it. There do not appear to have been radio mechanics stationed on gun sites at that time. They would presumably have been centred on the RAOC workshops.

It was early in 1941 that the War Office decided to give the King's Commission to radio officers, to simplify relationships with the Royal Artillery on site. Lt Col J. A. Radcliffe was still worried about maintaining high academic standards. He had wanted only men with first or second-class degrees in maths or physics or, strangely enough, in biology. He had seen the need for people who could be scientific observers and able to assess how improvement in operation could be brought about. However, by 1941, equipment was more reliable than it had been and some of the functions of the original officers had been taken over by an Operational Research Group, highly specialised. Radcliffe's successor at Petersham was J. A. Harrison who I think must have been the Headmaster when I did my radar officers' training in mid-1943.

The GLII (AA No. I Mark II) was in fairly general use by mid-1942 when I was working as a radar mechanic in Upton, Cheshire. I have described it elsewhere. Delivery of it started in early 1941 and was completed by August 1943. The Mark III (Canadian) came onto the gun sites in 1943 — ours at Hampstead, I think, in late autumn 43. New valve technology work by two British scientists in the first two years of war had enabled progress on the design of 10cm wave-length radars. They produced the cavity magnetron or resonator valve. We shared our knowledge of the invention with the Americans, who were later able to produce the 584 radar, the most successful of the war. This was used against V1s.

Although the officers on the Petersham course were taught about GL Mark I, I only encountered it once in my job as a radar maintenance officer. It had been superseded by Mark II by mid to late 1943 when I was posted to London. The one exception, if I remember rightly, was at Chequers, where there was a light Royal Artillery battery (all male) on Coombe Hill. I "stood in" for another RMO quite early on, for a few weeks and found rather a dusty radar set, which needed a bit of sprucing up by the solitary radar mechanic. Maybe it did not matter a great deal, as Chequers was never attacked by air. The battery went up to London, onto the roof of number 10 when the PM was in town. I doubt if the great man ever had time to go out to Coombe Hill, though he quite frequently visited the Hyde Park gun site when at Downing Street. He had a remarkable grasp of the technicalities of what was happening on a gun site during a raid. I suppose daughter Mary had briefed him. She was an ATS officer on the Hyde Park Gun Site.

When I first arrived at Hampstead, there were two pieces of radar equipment Mark II on site. They were the transmitter cabin, weighing six tons fifteen hundredweight and labelled TX, and the receiver cabin, RX, weighing five tons eight hundredweight. The TX worked at a voltage of 20,000 volts and ours sent out signals at a wave length of 56 mega cycles. When the signals hit a plane, they bounced back and were picked up by the RX. Radars on each gun site in London worked on different wave lengths.

I remember my first visit to the transmitter at Hampstead. In the corner was a mysterious wooden box. When I was told that it was gun-cotton, for blowing up the TX in case of invasion, I regarded it with great suspicion, knowing little about explosives. After a few months the box was removed, much to my relief.

At some stage in 1941/42, poultry farmers and everyone who kept chickens (half the population did) were badly put out by the fact that the country seemed to have run out of chicken-wire. No one knew why except the Government, which was not saying. The truth was that it was all being requisitioned for a strange contraption known as the GL mat. The research work that we did on different sites in 1942 – 43 at the 22nd Workshop Company in Upton was obviously helping to provide information for the planning of the mat, although we did not know it at the time. Blackett and his team in their research had found that it was necessary to mount the receiver cabin on an area of "even electrical properties". They had discovered that chicken-wire was the nearest to the ideal. They therefore invented the GL mat (gun-laying mat). Every mat consisted of a hexagon of more than 15,000 sq yards — radius 80 feet. Mats ranged in height from about one foot to nine feet, depending on ground conditions. On some gun sites the ground was relatively flat and on others it was decidedly wavy. I will not go into the technicalities of how these mats were constructed and supported, but once they were in position there were problems with grass and small shrubs which must not be allowed to grow up through them. Some battery commanders found they could run a mowing machine under their mat, or at least someone stooping with a pair of shears. One hapless CO I heard of had the brilliant idea of keeping geese (or was it ducks?) under his very low-lying mat. The mats were a continual headache on all gun sites.

In the middle of the mat, of course, there had to be a platform for the radar receiver, with a ramp under the mat to get it there. Then there had to be a wooden cat-walk, for personnel to reach it. There had to be a short ladder from ground to cat-walk. In pitch darkness, the journey could be a bit hazardous.

The two cabins could both be rotated towards the target plane and then aligned for the best response on the cathode ray tubes in the RX. The TX sent out signals which bounced back from the target and were picked up by the RX. There was a range aerial fairly low down on the outside of the cabin, two bearing aerials, one each side, and elevation aerials centrally above. Range, bearing and elevation were displayed on three cathode ray tubes in the cabin. The operator's job was to concentrate on keeping the signals on crosswires on the cathode ray tubes, each turning a handle as smoothly and accurately as possible. It is impossible to explain all the intricacies for the general reading public, but I cannot resist describing an ingenious system whereby on the bearing and elevation CRT there were fed in a "range-plus-bearing" and "range-minus-bearing" signal in two different colours, red and green, and the operators had the job of keeping these two equal. The same applied to elevation signals.

When on target, it was possible quickly to check that the equipment was not facing 180 degrees out (as it theoretically could be). If the guns started firing 180 degrees off target, it would not greatly have helped London defences.

Inside the cabin of the RX, high above the CRT for range, on the right, there was a small IFF tube — Identification Friend or Foe. Special IFF aerials were on the roof of the cabin. The IFF circuits sent out signals to be intercepted by our own FRIENDLY planes, either night-fighters or bombers returning home from a mission. Our pulses triggered a response signal in these planes and we could see a special blip on our IFF cathode ray tube. If there were no blip we could assume it was a FOE. No blip: no friend. Occasionally the crew of a plane would forget to switch on their IFF as they came home. If we fired, we certainly got an immediate response! It might be that they switched on their forgotten IFF, but there was a back up system of three coloured flares, which the plane put out in a certain order. Security was so good that the order of colours was changed each night. This meant there was zero chance of enemy bombers being "genned up" to the colour code.

The Canadian AA No.3 Mark I, a radar with 10cm aerials and cavity magnetron valve, came onto our site at Hampstead in late autumn 1943. It worked at 2,000 megacycles. We were lucky to have the most advanced version existing at that time, in which the set, once on target, could be switched to "automatic". This meant the human operators were eliminated, once the radar was on target, and accuracy did not depend on their having a steady hand and eye.

The range of the Canadian equipment was not as great as the AA No.1 Mark II, though its accuracy was greater. So the two different pieces of equipment worked in conjunction with each other — the Mark II acting as the Search and "putter on" for the Canadian set. The following of the target worked on the same principle as the Mark II, a "range-plus-bearing" and "minus-bearing", "range-plus-elevation" and minus. If one sat on the seat outside the cabin and looked through its telescope (which worked together with everything inside) one could see the plane on its centre cross-wire. If the set required adjusting, one could see the equipment was "hunting", that was swinging slightly to either side of centre. I will not try to initiate you into the mysteries of the "constant current valve" but continued checking or tuning of circuits was required.

I went to a girls' public school, Queenswood, in Hertfordshire. Queenswood happened to be almost next door to Brookman's Park, an early BBC relay station. We had lights-out at 9.00pm which was too early for me at the age of 13–14 years. To relieve the boredom of lying in bed in the dark, I took an "instrument" with me from home — my first technical instrument; a very simple one. Firstly, there was a square of plywood — about 5 inches a side: there was a crystal fastened to it: then there was a "cat's whisker": finally there was a small pair of earphones. After a bit of prodding the crystal with the cat's whisker reception was very clear and I enjoyed the programmes. Often there was good dance music — Henry Hall and so on. This contraption was concealed underneath my pants in my bottom drawer and I cannot remember how it escaped notice when we had Drawer Inspections, which we did fairly often, to make sure we were keeping our clothes folded properly and everything neat and tidy.

When our Canadian Mark III arrived at Hampstead gun site in 1943 I was fascinated to discover that the oscillator circuit worked with a crystal. The discovery took me back to my illicit wireless sessions in bed at school.

At Easy 22 the battery had been very fortunate indeed, before the Canadian Mark III was available, in having a "fine-tuned" radar which was the British equivalent. It was labelled British Mark III.2. Although it was designed and produced independently before the Canadian equipment, it was labelled 2 because there were delays in production. Hampstead had one of the first of these and it was a wonderful piece of engineering and superior to the Canadian model. I think it was made by Cossor and was not as fragile or vulnerable as the Canadian. At Easy 22 we had an excellent Corporal in charge of ours and it never went wrong. I seem to remember the Corporal telling me after a raid that the radar picked up a bomb and followed it almost all the way to earth. Sadly, although it was superior, once the Canadian radar was generally available we lost our beloved British Mark III. But we acquired a new electric predictor. I had always imagined that this was a secret piece of equipment. Then one day when someone in the Mess had bought a copy of the Illustrated London News, we found an article about it, with a description about how it worked and even illustrations of it. We were very indignant about this, but it transpired that it was an American invention and so I suppose we felt reluctantly that they had a right to give it publicity. I have to say that the Americans were not considered to be very security-conscious.

The forerunner, The Sperry predictor, was entirely mechanical and made a whirring noise when in action. When I was an undergraduate later I remember writing to an Ack-Ack friend that it was agony trying to write my first essay and, when I sat down to do it, my brain made a noise like a Sperry predictor.

The efficiency of anti-aircraft improved year by year, in spite of many circumstances militating against it. During the earlier major blitz, the anti-aircraft performance was greatly hampered by the fact that there were only about a fifth of the number of gun sites in action in London which had been planned. By 1943, Pile had fought so hard that he had succeeded in establishing a much more satisfactory number. But throughout the war he struggled to improve the radar, the predictor, the guns and their fuses. Towards the end of the war the sites got their proximity-fused ammunition which exploded on sensing the target — or anything else in the air. Many a poor little bird met an untimely end because of these shells.

Sir Frederick Pile fought battles continually against almost everyone from Churchill downwards. After Dunkirk nearly all branches of the services were short of manpower and inclined to try and filch some men from Ack-Ack. The navy were continually trying to recover some of the 5.25 guns which had been given to Ack-Ack Command. We had these at Primrose Hill and Mill Hill and they were so important because of their considerable range.

As I did my job, helping to keep the gun sites in action by keeping the radar in trim, I do not think I gave much thought, if any, to what the German defences were doing. I never tried to imagine what German radar might be like, although we were all aware of the appalling losses our bomber forces suffered. Recently I have read a little about what was going on in German anti-aircraft. Apparently German understanding of the principles governing the function of radio location began to develop soon after Watson Watt built his first experimental equipment in this country in the mid-1930s.

In the early days of the war, our Government and our senior service officers did not believe the Germans had any radio location equipment. It was not until R. D. Jones, the most senior intelligence researcher in the RAF, succeeded in obtaining photographs of Freya, not far from Cherbourg, that English officials were convinced that German radar existed.

Freya was not extended to a large number of sites in the early 1940s and German defences depended largely on searchlights and sound locators. Their success then and later in the mid-40s was due to the very considerable number of anti-aircraft guns: a much heavier concentration, apparently, than London defences were allowed during the Blitz. The Luftwaffe replaced Freya with an equipment called Würzburg which measured target height much more accurately. The Luftwaffe also had a number of instruments using infra-red radiation. Much has been written about German defences, but it was outside my sphere of knowledge during the war, so I will not dwell on it. It seems that the greater success of the British during the later years of the war was due to the splendid co-operation and continual consultation between our senior officers and our scientists. Much of this was certainly due to Churchill and the Germans were not so good at it.

When the resonator magnetron was introduced into our radar, both in anti-aircraft and in our planes, night fighters and bombers, there was great concern lest Germany should get hold of it. However, when a bomber was eventually shot down by the Germans sufficiently intact for them to examine the magnetron, the Germans, for some unknown reason, did not take advantage of this discovery and never used the magnetron in their later radar sets.

CHAPTER
NINE

Everyday Work on Radar

After describing the radar, I thought I would have a go at detailing what radar mechanics, NCOs and radar officers did in working hours (which could be any hours of the twenty-four, round the clock).

One of the first things the mechanics had to learn was how to by-pass the safety gadgets which were built into the Mark II equipment. Theoretically, when one took the back off the receiver, the voltage on the circuits was cut off, so that no one could get an electric shock when dabbling about inside the set. Of course there were many occasions when one needed to get inside the set, among the transformers and backs of cathode ray tubes. All power had to be off then. But there were equally many occasions when the mechanic had to see which valves were not lighting up when they should or needed to test the voltage on certain circuits. At that point the crocodile clips which everyone carried came into play, shorting out the safety devices. Occasionally, of course, a moment's carelessness gave one a 4,000 volt shock. I remember having one. That was why we all wore rubber soles on our boots, so that no great harm was done.

Looking back on my "other ranks" days, I remember that the girls had an advantage over the men. Being smaller, we were able to fit into nooks and crannies inside the sets. I had an additional advantage. Born left-handed, but made to write and do some other things with my right hand, I became ambidextrous, or what I called "perverted and sinister" (perverted sinistral). In odd corners I could use right or left hands equally well, to hold wires or screw bolts. This was particularly useful when making modifications to the receiver, as we often had to do at Upton.

We were working in the days before transistors, and thermionic valves were very apt to go wrong. They went "soft", often glowing blue. Sometimes good daily maintenance could anticipate trouble and prevent it happening during a raid. Time-delays on switches could get stuck. Brushes on motors or other rotating parts could become dirty or greasy. The very large insulators on the big VT98 transmitter valves had to be kept spotless. Insulation on the IFF aerials was inclined to get damp in the early days and had to be dried out. The main aerial leads were sheathed in lead and this cracked, causing trouble. Any condenser, resistor or switch or soldered connection could cause trouble. Diagnosis of trouble on the radar required a knowledge of the function of every single component. The odd kick to one of the panels often did wonders.

The radar mechanics and NCOs on my five gun sites were responsible for all the daily maintenance and for "first aid" in the case of faults causing the equipment to malfunction. If they could not fix it, they got on the telephone to me. I would say, "Have you tried this?" or "Have you tried that?" My job was to advise, diagnose or in urgent cases to go over to the gun site in trouble. In extreme cases we would take the offending section out (like a metal drawer with circuits on it), take it into workshops and replace it with a tested drawer from the REME workshop at Park Royal. Meanwhile, the battery was informed that the radar was out of action. This meant that the gun site was out of action and the guns could not fire. So it was serious! The REME team then had to work on the problem until it was solved, however many hours it took — sometimes all night.

Churchill once said to Rooseveld, "Give us the tools and we'll finish the job." Radar mechanics said, "Give us the job and we'll finish the tools." The mechanics were a cheerful lot. I hardly ever remember them becoming irritated or depressed when things did not go well. I never heard a swear word from any of them. Having been at a girls' public school until June 1939, I did not realise how extraordinary that was. The relationship between us was really good, respectful but affectionate. The cartoon they pinned on my office wall tells it all!

My good friend Martyn Clark at the REME Museum has from time to time sent me articles on the history and workings of radar, against which I could check my memory. One article above all stimulated and amused me. It was a sort of diary, "Recollections of a RMO" by Major General V Metcalfe MA, CEng, FIEE etc. It described his experience in 1942–43 in Felixstowe and his previous period of training in

Cambridge and Petersham. This was just over a year before I started working at Hampstead. What amazed me about his diary as a radar maintenance officer was how similar our experiences had been. Almost every paragraph struck a chord with me and I said to myself, "Me, too!" I was extremely badly tempted to incorporate his diary into this book as a chapter. It would have saved me such a lot of work!! (I am joking of course.) I do not know whether Major General Metcalfe is still alive, but if so I say, "Snap." In my less sane moments I ventured to conjecture whether, if I had stayed in the army after the war, I would now be a Major General. Of course, I would not. I was not bright enough and could never have passed all those examinations.

There were some weekly tests which RMOs had to perform. One was to take a small oscillator in a box with an aerial round each of the gun sites. It had to be switched on some yards from the receiver cabin and the RX rotated until it was "on target". Sitting on the seat on the outside of the cabin, one then had to check, through the telescope sited there, that the visual and electronic readings coincided. Any error had to be within very strict limits and a report on the situation went into headquarters each week. This was one of the tasks that RMOs took on for their fellow RMOs when the latter were on leave or sick. Luckily I never found any errors requiring action. I had more than a suspicion that some of my fellow RMOs forged their findings when I was away.

A regular happening on the sites was a visit from the Inspection Team. They were highly skilled people, organised by Ack-Ack command. In one way they were welcome because on the day of their visit the radar had to be officially put out of action and parts of the radar which we normally could not reach were examined and tested. Everything was scrutinised, right down to knobs and paint work and a full official report was made on each piece of equipment. The only snag was that quite frequently after they had departed we found that something had been left unconnected or a valve half in its socket. Our staff had to check and re-check before the evening brought a possible air raid. I was amused to find a passage in Major General Metcalfe's diary, "*Saturday 26th September* H3: Inspection Pary set LO on wrong dip; current of 160μA compared with 212μA on my setting. This was not the only occasion when I had to make adjustments after a workshop inspection party left one of my sites. But by this time I had over four months of hands-on experience with GL Mk2 and I had sufficient confidence to overrule workshop staff. However, I had tremendous respect for and confidence in the artificers who came out to investigate faults I could not clear myself." (Artificers being the Staff Sergeants)

Fairly soon after my posting to E22, I was informed by the powers-that-be that the radar on the site was due for calibration. Being newly qualified I was rather cocky and not too much daunted by the thought. Having informed Arthur Gough, the Battery Commander, what had to be done, I set about making the arrangements.

The Royal Artillery made provision for the necessary ATS girls to be on the command post to take readings from the predictor and other instruments. The radar operators — three of them — were detailed for the radar set. I had a telephone number for Croydon airfield and a squadron leader's name. In the morning, bright and early, I got on the telephone. A cheerful voice answered me, friendly and obviously intending to be helpful. There was a momentary element of surprise because this radar officer turned out to be a woman but the squadron leader took that in his stride and my reception was of normal efficiency and politeness. Yes, he could supply an aircraft for the Hampstead gun site that day. Communications with the plane were to be by code letters laid out on the ground, as they could not supply a wireless operator. Pause. Then came the crunch question, "What is the height of the clouds over with you?" "Er, um," I said, "I'm not sure". "Well just poke your head out of the office door," he said patiently, "and give me a figure." "I have to confess I wouldn't be any wiser," I said. "It wasn't in my training course." He laughed. After that, of course, I learned to consult the ATS spotters on the command post before telephoning to book a plane from Croydon. They knew about clouds. We did not have a Michael Fish available during the war.

One afternoon Easy 22 were asked to take part in an exercise which was in a sense a test of the Canadian equipment. The radar was to be manned to await the arrival of an "unusually fast" plane. The powers-that-be wanted to know whether the Mark 3 C could pick up and follow this unidentified plane. I thought it would be fun to sit on the outside seat at the end of the cabin and watch the exercise through the telescope linked to the radar. If the equipment was not properly adjusted, one could watch it swing slightly right and left of the target. This was called hunting. In this instance, everything was well tuned and after a short period I saw the plane we were waiting for appear on the cross-wire in the telescope. It certainly was odd looking and in the fairly short time before it had passed over and out of our range I got the impression of a double fuselage. This was, in fact, a plane with a twin-beam (carrying the tail unit). Some recent research has convinced me that it was probably the second jet-engine fighter plane, the second prototype De Havilland D.H. 100 Vampire F Mark I. I cannot recall exactly when we were asked to test our ability to follow it, but I imagine it would have been the second prototype because our Canadian radar was the automatic model and I do not think we had it in September 1943, when the first prototype flew. I owe confirmation of the identification of this "mystery plane" to a member of staff at the REME Museum who recently transferred from RAF Museum, Hendon.

We were told nothing about the plane we had seen and followed. It was highly secret. As far as I can remember we managed to hold it in our sights very well and were rather pleased with ourselves.

One task which had to be undertaken daily was "Checking dials". This usually happened in the early evening and meant every piece of equipment had to be manned. The information on the radar, of course, had to be passed on instantaneously to all other parts of the gun site. The dials were connected by cables and the system, known as the magslips, worked very simply with induction coils. If there was damp in any connections, or any other insulation problem, the dials would be giving a mis-reading. I think "Checking dials" was carried out entirely by Royal Artillery personnel but a radar mechanic or predictor mechanic always had to be available in case there were problems.

Another evening task was the setting-in of ballistic correction. This was done on a dial in the receiver. The trajectory of a shell on leaving the gun is never an absolutely straight line. It is curved and the curve depends on weather conditions — temperature, humidity etc. A ballistic reading was telephoned through to every gun site each evening. Perhaps this will serve to indicate some of the intricacies of the struggle to achieve accuracy in firing. Another area outside the radar mechanic's control concerned fusing of the shells. Through the 1940s there were many experiments and modifications with this and by 1943 greatly improved accuracy in firing.

Early one evening one of our faithful Lister generators packed up and we could not do without it. The problem was beyond the capacity of our radar mechanics or me, so appeals were made to the Park Royal workshop. They immediately sent out a generator mechanic. After he had been left in peace for an hour or so, I decided to go and see how he was getting on and find out what was the diagnosis. There was a canvas tarpaulin fringe round the roof of the open-sided shed. As I approached in the dusk I said to the oil-smeared figure within: "Good evening. How long do you think this is likely to take?" All he could see of me was a pair of khaki trousers, boots and a leather jerkin. "Come 'ere, young and beautiful," he said. "Why do you want to know? Thought you would be pleased to have a rest." "Well," I said in my most crushing tone (seldom used), "I happen to be Miss Inkster the radar officer and I want us to get the site in action again as soon as we can." Profuse apologies from the poor man! Luckily he was a good mechanic and all repairs were done before dark. We did have a raid later that night.

Our work in Hampstead and on the other gun sites was bound up closely with the work that went on in the two REME workshops at Park Royal and Loughton. Brigadier "Sandy" Gordon in an article "REME in Ack-Ack Command 1955" says: "Throughout the war workshops were required to work very long hours manufacturing special equipment and fitting it on site, frequently during air raids. The Workshops at Park Royal were working day and night on modifications in 1940 with bombs falling all round and part of the shop was set on fire."

The whole REME Workshop in Minerva Road, Park Royal was an extensive area, rather like a series of hangars, containing sections which dealt with guns, transport, tools and equipment large and small, and radar. Some of it was in the ruins of bombed-out factories. My memory says, "Cosmetics Factory", but I cannot remember which! The radar Workshop was in its own hutted section which included its own extensive stores. The captain in charge of radar work, a delightful Welshman, had his own office. There were several highly-skilled staff sergeants working in the radar field, ready to give specialist advice or if necessary to go out to gun sites; though by 1943, this was seldom necessary because sites were lucky enough to have their own permanent REME staff coping with maintenance, repairs and emergencies of all kinds.

When I look back on the Park Royal Workshops, I am filled with admiration for the way it was run and for its professionalism. Everyone was generous with practical help or technical advice. I would go into Workshops for an hour or two, perhaps once a week, to consult where a gun site was encountering problems or to collect perhaps a new panel for a radar set or small parts, including replacement valves. The logistics for supplying radar sets must have been a headache for administrators at all levels. (Red Book) "The number of major items of test gear alone . . . ran into some 9,500 separate items and the minor items certainly excelled that number."

CHAPTER
TEN

Air Raids

Easy-two-two had early warning of the approach of enemy bombers. There was information coming through to us as soon as the planes left the French coast. The range of A.A.No.1.Mark2 was 60,000 yards and there had been earlier warning from Command HQ. Generators were switched on. Alarm bells rang on the site and in the officers' mess and their noise was deafening. ATS girls turned out with battle dress over pyjamas, curlers in hair under tin hats, to man the radar, predictors and other instruments on the Command Post. The gunners manned the artillery. As I lay in bed in the Officers' Mess I heard the large generators being switched on and waited for the bells to ring. I made a habit of getting up immediately and flung on necessary clothing. I remember one occasion early in the night when we had not yet gone to bed. I was in the middle of washing my hair and I jammed my tin hat on top of my wet hair. Water dripped down my back most uncomfortably during the raid.

The ATS officers who shared my bedroom were on duty from the word "go" and probably one of them would be acting as Gun Position Officer. I was filled with admiration at the speed with which they all got dressed and got over to the Command Post to watch for the radar to get on target and selected bomber to come within firing range. The person on duty actually shouted "Fire" to the guns over the intercom. That was as near to aggressive action and "the kill" as any woman got during the war.

I had to be ready for action if the radar needed attention. Generally I positioned myself in the receiver cabin, with the three ATS operators. I would stand next to the range operator's screen. One could watch the "signal" in the form of a pulse coming in and would brace oneself for a colossal bang as the guns opened fire as soon as the plane came within their range at 14,000 yards. Sometimes I went to the Command Post, where I could watch the large squared screen and could see the target approaching. One could tell how the radar was performing quite well from that position. The atmosphere in the Command Post during firing was absolutely electric. After the plane had either passed on, was fired on or retreated, the radar receiver swung round to the Search position and the whole process started again. Meanwhile, shrapnel was coming down and the revolting smell of cordite was all-pervasive. Window also came down but was not dangerous. Shrapnel was. One of the ATS spotters in Hampstead was blinded when a piece of shrapnel bounced off the low concrete wall round the Command Post and into her eye.

How shall I describe the noise of the guns when one was on the site? It was an assault on the ears: more than that . . . it was as if one had been bashed over the head. The poet Doyle spoke of the "all shattering guns". It was a crashing, bellowing, hammering on one's head: a blasting, crushing, tearing sound: a skull-splitting series of explosions. How the ATS radar and predictor operators kept their hands steady on their handles, as they stayed on target, I do not know. Later on, the automatic transmission on our Canadian radar Mark III which came in Autumn 1943 gave for much greater accuracy. However well trained and cool-headed the operators were, they could never achieve the same smoothness of operation which was necessary in transmission to the guns.

Recently on a National Trust cruise round Britain, I met a passenger who had been a radar operator in the North East of England. The thing she remembered most was the sound of the guns. She said that as a child she had always hated Guy Fawkes night. Like me, she had dreaded fireworks parties and tried to avoid them if possible. And we both found ourselves on gun sites during the war!

One night in particular I remember as the Incendiaries Night. A short while after the raids started, the sky became quite spectacular. There was a strange rain falling from Heaven — a rain of fire. As the incendiaries left the planes and broke away from their breadbaskets, they each traced a line of light in the blue night sky: like spangles: like tresses of hair gleaming in the dark: like falling stars: a brilliant firework display — it seemed from horizon to horizon. We were told that Alistair Simm's house was burned to the ground that night. I have to confess I foolishly lingered in the open air that night, because the scene was so beautiful. Eventually I decided reluctantly to go across to the radar receiver to see if all was well.

The German's used a good number of incendiaries. One night a "breadbasket" of incendiaries came down intact — not separating as they should have done in air. They made quite a display and burned an immense hole in the ground near the ATS sleeping quarters. No attempt was made to put that big bonfire out, as it would have been nigh impossible.

One raid I remember vividly. Guns were firing when I went over the cat-walk to the radar receiver. I would have had to await the right moment when the door next to the range operator was accessible, as the cabin rotated on its turntable. I nipped in. A few minutes later, the ATS corporal in charge of the team must have received a message over her earphones from the Battery Commander or the gun position officer in the Command Post. She said, "Ma-am, would you please look out and see what it's like out there?" I opened the door. As the radar was on target, the corporal could not take her eyes off the screen. Outside it was like a sea of fire. Dozens of incendiaries had fallen through the gun-laying mat and were cheerfully lighting up the ground around us. I took one look and hurriedly shut the door. "Everything is fine," I said breezily. By the time the raid was over, the bombs had burned themselves out and — miracle of miracles — none had fallen on the wooden roof of the cabin or on the wooden cat-walk. The next morning at breakfast time the battery commander, Arthur Gough, was so intrigued by what had happened that he sent men to count the number of incendiary shells which had fallen through the mat. There were between 40 and 50. Sir Frederick Pile described this incident in his book, "Ack-Ack", but remembered it wrongly as happening in the Thames estuary. It was not in the estuary. It was at Hampstead and happened at the end of January 1944.

During one raid, I had to go up to Whetstone Park. As we sped up the Finchley Road, there was a piercing whistle and a thud which sounded quite close to the road. An hour later, as we were counting on getting home quickly, we found ourselves frustrated. There was a barrier right across the road and a large notice "unexploded bomb". We had to make quite a long detour, but we did not mind. We just thanked our lucky stars that it had been "unexploded".

I mentioned "window" earlier on. This was a code name for a device designed to upset radar and was used by both sides. Ours consisted of strips of black paper, coated on one side with aluminium foil, 30cm long and 1.5cm wide. This was half the wavelength of the German radar and had the effect of disturbing the signals being received by the radar. When the German planes used it on us, it looked as if there were dozens of planes in addition to the one we were trying to target. These signals bobbed about and seemed to be coming in at different speeds. Our little radar operators found it difficult to follow the true signal through this fuzz, but I think generally managed extraordinarily well.

The idea of window, which the Germans called "düppel" had been known to both sides quite early in the war, but not used by either for fear of retaliation. During the summer of 1943, however, British bomber losses were so great (275 in June 1943) that we were driven to use window and it was used in vast quantities during the Hamburg raids in July and Ruhr raids in August. Our bomber losses were cut to about 3%. From then on, the Germans used their "düppel" and more and more complicated means were devised by both sides, to defeat interference.

During the launch of Overlord on D-Day we used powerful radar-jamming equipment, but window was also used in a brilliant exercise, Operation Taxable. To deceive the Germans about the direction in which our invasion force was heading, No. 617 Squadron was employed to drop window in a complicated pattern. The famous "Dambusters" Squadron flying to and fro in precise timing threw out vast quantities of window, one flight behind another in exact sequence, creating an illusion of hundreds of ships on German radar screens. The Germans were tricked into concentrating on a non-existent fleet apparently moving away from Normandy. Similar exercises along the Somme, diverted German defences away from the real invasion targets.

I had arrived at Hampstead in early autumn just in time to settle in before more intensive raids started again. The Germans had been badly hit by our heavy bombing of Hamburg, so their retaliative raids were nicknamed "The Scalded Cat Raids". A very few fighter-bombers had played around on our coastline in the summer. Then on the night of 7th – 8th October 1943 London was attacked by more than 60 of them, flying faster and higher than any had done before. The gun sites did not do well on that particular night. The newly-arrived Canadian GL3 and on some sites new electrical predictors meant that the Royal Artillery staff were still unused to the equipment.

On 17th October, a solid week of raids on London and the Home Counties began. The bombers were Junkers 88, accompanied by fighter-bombers. There were many flares and a great deal of window, though Canadian radar was scarcely affected by that. Nevertheless, as Pile records, our anti-aircraft "kills" and "damaged" totals were considerably better than in 1942. The amount of practice these raids gave to our personnel paid off later, as the battery was better prepared when there was a raid on London on the night of January 21–22. There were 200 bombers — the greatest number for nearly three years. It was as bad as some of the worst attacks during the 1940–41 Blitz. The bombers were identified as Dorniers, Heinkels, Messerschmitts, Junkers and Focke-Wulf. The raids came in two waves that night. The first was just after dinner, 8 o'clock-ish. The second was between 4 and 5 in the morning and lasted about an hour. By that date the Inner Artillery Zone (IAZ) had sixteen 5.25 guns. fifty-three London batteries engaged them and only 12% of their bombs fell on London, so there were comparatively few casualties. They did carry some "nasties" including parachute bombs, phosphorous bombs, some "heavies" and explosive incendiaries, so it was a good thing not many got through to London. Firing by our batteries was very heavy, which was why most of the bombers turned away before reaching London. Only one fifth penetrated the defences and of those London Ack-Ack shot down eight and the RAF eight. Churchill wrote a letter of congratulation.

At the end of January 1944, there was another heavy raid, aimed at the London docks. Of 130 bombers, only a third got through, but many incendiaries were dropped. That was the night of the fires in the GL Mat round our radar receiver.

Raids again on 3rd February and eight others before mid-March. Although the bombers visited other cities after that, including Bristol, Portsmouth and Plymouth, they returned to London on 13th February. There were 230 bombers, but although they carried over 160 tons of bombs, they only succeeded in dropping 4 tons on their target. By May 1944, after much practice, Ack-Ack Command kills rose to 10%. There were two bad nights on 18th and 20th February when they dropped 250 tons on London.

Recalling the Hamburg raids reminded me of a jolly little ditty in Punch. Practically every night on the BBC News there had been reference to our heavy raids on "the marshalling yards at Hamm". It seemed to go on for weeks. The little poem went like this:-
"Oh, what a disaster!
I have been made station master
At Hamm.
OH DAMN!!"

Although we laughed at that little rhyme, none of us felt what the Germans call Schadenfreude — delight in suffering (that is, other people's suffering). When we were reasonably sure that Easy 22 had scored a hit and destroyed a German plane, Arthur Gough, our CO, turned to me and said, "Poor devils!" There was no gloating there: no triumphalism.

But there was another aspect to this. When our anti-aircraft shot down their invading bombers and killed their airmen, someone in Germany was bereft. There were mixed feelings about people on both sides, in the air, in the cities and in the countryside. We felt for our own men who died in their planes, either in Germany or in this country. We felt for German fliers, burning in their fighters or bombers over England. We felt for civilians in great cities in the terror of bombing raids, here or on the continent. We felt for families on both sides deprived forever of sons, husbands or lovers. But during the war our sympathies for our enemies had to be kept tightly in rein and our justified anger for what the Germans had brought about had to be the predominant emotion.

Christabel Bielenberg, an English woman married to a German in the mid-30s and living in Germany throughout the war, wrote in her book "The Past is Myself" most movingly and poetically about the effects of the war on the small community in the Black Forest where she took refuge from the horrific Berlin bombing in 1944.

"Rohrbach was a little world, an unimportant world, which had no say whatsoever in affairs of state, but still had to carry the burden of Hitler's dreams of conquest.

There were no young men in the farmhouses up and down the valley and every day the little local newspaper, while dutifully splashing huge headlines of superlatives on its front page, reserved for the back page the news which affected the villagers most. Alois — Conrad Smolensk — the Dnieper Basin — my loving and diligent husband — our dearly beloved son — in stillem Schmerz — in tiefer Trauer — in silent pain — in deepest mourning. Simple records of a soldier dying in a far off land, his death reverberating back to some lonely farmhouse, where from then on there would be no strong hand to turn the stony sod or wield the axe."

Casualties among our airmen flying over Britain occurred from time to time. Sometimes the complicated interweaving of gunfire and night fighters failed to ensure the safety of the fighters. Occasionally, no doubt, there were failures of IFF (Identification Friend or Foe) either in ground radar or in plane. Sometimes fighters collided with each other or they were shot down by German fighter-bombers. The John Pudsey poem still moves me deeply.

"Do not despair
For Johnny head-in-air
He sleeps as sound
As Johnny underground

Better by far
For Johnny the bright-star
To keep your head
And see his children fed."

Re-reading this poem in later years, two lines take on a significance they would not have had for me in war-time. While we were at ground level and our planes were in the sky, far below toiled the Bevan boys of whom I knew nothing at the time. So many of them also died. They were conscripted: many would have preferred to be in the air, rather than in the dark bowels of the earth. "Johnny underground" indeed.

I do not think I realised at the time the complexity of the juggling act which had to be performed at Stanmore. I knew, of course, that there were times when we could have fired, but were not allowed to, because our own fighters were overhead. My brother was one of them in a Beaufighter. The civilian population was angry with us when we did not fire. The more noise we made, the more impressed people were.

The more accurate the shooting of the gun sites became, the higher the German bombers had to fly and therefore the less accurate their bombing became. Intensive, accurate firing caused them to turn tail before reaching the centre of London. In the command post there was enormous satisfaction in watching bombers being plotted coming in, then seeing them turn tail and retreat. Generally they jettisoned their bombs on the villages so this was not popular either! Many of the bombers coming direct from Germany flew in over the Wash and flew south from there towards London.

CHAPTER
ELEVEN

People on the Site

It might not be appropriate to name all the people I can remember on the Hampstead gun site and the other gun sites with which I was associated. I shall try to draw some word-pictures, including some of the REME personnel, without giving too many names.

Among the Royal Artillery people, I did not get to know the gunners, because we hardly ever met, except occasionally at the station dances. I got to know the battery sergeant major, because of his kindness in driving me over to one of the other sites during a raid, when my truck and driver were not available. There was REME staff sergeant Tansley who joined our detachment when the Canadian Mark III came on site. I was filled with admiration for his knowledge and skill. The staff sergeants were exceptionally well trained — I believe at Arborfield — and knew more about the equipment than I did. They generally were slightly older and had had experience in electrical work in pre-war days. There was another REME sergeant on E22, sergeant Bowden, who had been a policeman in Birmingham before the war. He was a delightful person, cheerful and imperturbable and I could imagine him in the police of pre-war days.

At the next level down, there was a splendid corporal who, before I arrived, had managed the maintenance of the British GL Mark III single-handed. This was an excellent piece of equipment which never went wrong and followed targets faultlessly. After one raid, he described to me how the Mark III locked on to a bomb and followed it down — luckily landing not too near us. Unfortunately the powers-that-be took this British equipment away from us when the Canadian one arrived. I got the REME workshop to arrange for him to receive his third stripe when he left us.

Another corporal came to work on the Canadian equipment on Willy 14. The magnetron valve with a very high voltage on it was on the roof, with a special cover over it. The corporal had had the cover off, in order to check the electrical circuit underneath. He turned round at some point, lost his balance and fell over backwards. He sat on the magnetron. The voltage could have killed him but it didn't. He was thrown off the roof onto the ground, fifteen feet below. Amazingly he was unhurt, though I would imagine a little surprised. I heard about it the following day, but to my astonishment he was back at work behaving normally.

I think it was the same corporal whom I was able to help through a very difficult period. One day when I visited the off site I noticed he did not look his usual cheerful self, but nothing was said about it. Next time I went, he looked positively green. "What the devil is the matter with you?" I asked. It turned out that his wife was pregnant for the first time and the baby was overdue. His wife was extremely nervous and wanted him with her. He had used up all his annual leave and 48-hour leaves. I cannot remember what the situation would have been about compassionate leave but for some reason he could not get it. There is a phenomenon called the couvade in which a husband goes through something like labour pains at the same time as the wife. In some primitive societies he is put to bed and treated as if he were giving birth. This poor man was obviously going through something equivalent but prematurely. A normally imperturbable, sensible and reliable man was "in a state" and something had to be done about it. I said, "Go home and we will cover for you." So he went without an official pass — to be back in 48 hours without fail. I, being young, was quite anxious about this because I did not think the Royal Artillery officers would be too pleased if they knew. I held my breath until a day-and-a-half later, when he telephoned to tell me that the baby had arrived — "mother and son doing well". He returned to work that evening transformed. So I learnt in my young adult years what some men go through when their wives are about to produce a baby.

Another member of staff I remember with some affection. When our first electronic predictor arrived (late 1943 or early 1944) we gained a new member of staff, Cyril Blackman. I had been sent on a short course, involving trigonometric theories dimly remembered from school days — a week at Kidbrooke Workshops, our REME workshop south of the Thames. I am sure I could not have diagnosed anything but the simplest faults on that predictor. Cyril Blackman was the expert. He was very bright intellectually and, personality-wise, great fun. He contributed much to our enjoyment of the work we were all doing. It was he who pinned up on my office wall the cartoon to be found with my photographs. I kept it because it epitomised something of the officer/other-rank relationship in our team. There was humour and an appreciation of where responsibility lay.

There was a craftsman (REME equivalent of private) on the home site who was the only member of the REME detachment who gave me cause for concern. He was rather slapdash about his work on the Mark II radar. He lived locally and was inclined to slip off home at the least opportunity. Never rude to me, he adopted a slightly sulky attitude. There was something more serious, though, about what he did. In the transmitter, all the circuit diagrams were in a slim, hard-backed blue book chained to the equipment and kept on a shelf inside it. One day I noticed that the book was missing. When I asked where it had gone he denied all knowledge. I expressed displeasure and, as it was a security problem, I reported immediately to my REME headquarters. When questioned further, he said he had taken it off its chain because he wanted to study the circuits. When told to return it pretty-damn-quick, he said he had been worried because I had discovered it was missing, had panicked and had burnt it. My seniors said there was nothing we could do about it and gave us a new book. He was withdrawn from E22 shortly afterwards. I felt uneasy about the whole affair, as I did not trust him and felt he might have engaged in some traitorous activity.

A craftsman on my most northerly site was a different cause for anxiety. He was a very conscientious radar mechanic, liked by the others, who began to worry about him because he was developing such terrible headaches. Once or twice when I called in to that site he was working: sometimes he was not and the others said he was lying down. Once he looked fairly normal. Next time he looked as if he was in considerable pain and I sent him off duty to lie down. I was concerned about him but he said the medical officer was looking after him.

All this developed over quite a short period, but I was about to arrange to go and see the MO to suggest a referral to a consultant. Then, one morning, there was a telephone call. Our young mechanic had gone to a swimming bath with friends early in the morning. He had been diving and suddenly collapsed in the water. Apparently he suffered a major stroke and within minutes he had died. A post mortem revealed that the cause of the problems was an aneurysm in his brain.

Because the radar mechanics were attached to the Royal Artillery their medical records were held by them. On this young man's death, his documents had to be returned to his REME company. They were handed to me for onward transmission. Naturally I examined them and was dismayed to find that the medical officer had not taken the headache seriously. There was a comment: "In my opinion, this man should be treated with scant sympathy." I was very glad I had not read this comment a fortnight earlier, as it might have influenced the way I treated him. In fact he got maximum sympathy and support from me and from his colleagues, because we knew what sort of person he was.

This man's funeral was held at Brookwood Cemetery. I went down with my MO, Miles Salmon. He was a captain with an advisory role over all radar maintenance officers north of the river. This was the first funeral I had attended and I was very distressed but managed to stay controlled. Brookwood had a wonderful atmosphere, though I felt overwhelmed by the sheer size of it. The ceremony was impressive, with full military honours — gunfire over the grave.

Having six gun sites to be involved in, I had to have my own truck and driver. At first, I had Rigby, an ex-lorry driver, who was a real treasure. He was always there when wanted, and never seemed to mind if I was detained half the night at a site away from home. He looked after me like a father and on cold winter nights produced a rug to be tucked in round my knees. Unfortunately, after about two months he was transferred to other work and I was given Hawkins, an ex-parlour maid. I was then confronted with a problem. The gun sites were spread over quite a large area of North London. We were not allowed to carry maps and there were no signposts. One could not stop and ask passers-by the way to the local gun site. So we had to rely on my almost non-existent bump of locality. Somehow we made it.

I think it was Hawkins who drove me one eventful night during an air raid. We needed a replacement panel for the radar at Willy-One-Four. I rang Park Royal Workshop and was told they could help. When we got there, however, the panel had been tested and found wanting. The only "Good-un" was at Loughton Workshop, near Epping. So we had to brave the North Circular. Our road was lit by flares from planes overhead. We passed a small hospital ablaze on the left: then a broken gas main with spectacular flames shooting up on high. Then (and I never saw it again) a succession of incendiaries which had gone straight down into the tarmac of the North Circular and were sparkling away in great style. Hawkins drove through these with great aplomb, skilfully weaving left and right to avoid them. I think the raid was over by the time we got to Loughton, but it had been quite a journey.

I got on well with Hawkins, but unfortunately she was posted elsewhere after a few months. My next driver was a little Danish girl, who had a Norwegian boyfriend. Apparently they could understand each other perfectly well. While waiting for me at one of my ports of call, she would sit in the utility truck knitting happily. She had no book of patterns but made up her own as she went using an array of gorgeous colours. I longed to get her to knit me a jacket, but unfortunately I had no wool from pre-war days: all supplies were destroyed in the bombing of my home. My very few civilian clothing coupons could not be spared so, alas, I never got my Danish knitted jacket. As my driver she did not last very long. One sunny morning we were bowling along the North Circular on our way to Park Royal Workshops and, fortunately, were getting quite near. Suddenly the utility truck started going bumpty-bump, bumpty-bump. I said, "This is a puncture!" So we stopped and the driver got out. She came in again with a look of horror on her face. It was not a puncture! It was much worse! She had done some maintenance on the truck that morning and had had the wheels off. She had not tightened the screws properly on one wheel when she replaced it. The thread had been stripped completely. Luckily we got a lift from a REME lorry into workshops. The transport department people were *not* pleased with my little Dane. She was on a charge. I had to have a replacement truck and she was also replaced on the spot.

There was another driver crisis. The officer in charge of the radar workshop got in touch with me one day and explained that one of the sergeants was up for promotion to staff sergeant. He asked me if I would take him on, on probation for a month, as they were a little doubtful about his suitability. They would like a report from me as to how he got on. Of course I agreed, so I took him back with me to Easy 22. After a week, I was not too much impressed, as he seemed rather irresponsible. Then one evening after dinner, there was a raid. I got a telephone message from Friern Barnet saying that a magnetron valve had failed and I needed to go over with a replacement. I rang for my driver and truck, but they were nowhere to be found. A REME radar mechanic told me with embarrassment that this wretched staff sergeant on trial had taken his girlfriend out for the evening in my truck. He had had the cheek to tell my driver that he could go out for the evening too. I exploded!!!

I had to turn to the Battery Commander for help, because I had to get to the other gun site urgently. As it happened the CO's driver was not available. The only person who *was* available was the battery sergeant-major. So the BSM in the CO's truck took me over to the other site. When we got there, the guns were firing intermittently. The BSM drove me as near to the command post as he dared, as he was afraid his windscreen might be shattered. I had to report to the gun position officer in the command post before I went to the radar. As I walked under the guns, they started firing again and I felt as though something had hit me over the head. My ears went zing, ing, ing, ing — the first and only time I experienced what people call "ears ringing".

The next day there was a confrontation with the would-be REME staff sergeant. I reported what had happened to my REME major. The culprit was required to appear before him and given a thorough dressing-down. He forfeited his promotion and I am not sure he did not lose his third stripe. He certainly deserved to. This was the only disciplinary problem I had in the detachment. As I had not got to know the man, I felt no regrets: only indignation!

The team of REME radar mechanics were a smart bunch. I do not think it my imagination, but the winters of those war-time years were much colder than more recent ones. Like all good soldiers, our craftsmen knew how to make life bearable for themselves. On W9, close to the radar, they had been allocated a Nissen hut in which they spent the greater part of the day and often much of the night. Much cleaning of radar parts went on there and, if there was a fault on the equipment, if possible a detachable panel would be brought in to be tested and repaired. Often there was some intricate soldering of parts to be done. It was difficult to handle test-equipment, spanners and drills with frozen fingers. There was, of course, an allocation of fuel to the hut, to keep the ancient iron stove going — but never enough.

One day I dropped in to see them as I did at least once weekly. We were discussing how the radar had been performing during the previous night's raid. We talked of shortages of spares, of tools, of men. While the conversation was going on, I registered the fact that one of the team had whipped a large sack out of the corner of the workshop and withdrawn quietly with it. After a few minutes I noticed some surreptitious glances at wrist-watches and began to wonder whether I was out staying my welcome. However, I had no intention of cutting short my visit as I wanted to look at the equipment.

After about fifteen minutes, the man with the sack returned, the sack now being very lumpy and obviously heavy. Nothing more was said at the time. On two or three successive visits, I noticed that expeditions with the sack occurred strictly at the same time mid-morning. I was almost certain the men would not be pinching fuel from the battery store. Relationships with me were good, so eventually I was trusted with an explanation of what was going on. A railway line ran along one side of the gun site, immediately outside the perimeter fence. A train was due to pass a certain point at 11.15am. Corporal Janes suggested I should go down to watch the embankment a minute or two before that time. The train arrived punctually — they did in those days. It stopped and the stoker started shovelling fuel as fast as he could on to the embankment. A khaki figure stood waiting with a sack. Whether this was originally an arrangement with family connections or had developed more or less by accident I do not know. I never asked.

Sad and awful things happened at W9 as well. During one of the raids in the Autumn of 1943, a bomb fell between the Command Post and the radar transmitter. A large section of it went right through the transmitter, cutting off the radar mechanic's arm at the shoulder and killing him instantly. The little ATS operator turning the handles was unhurt. This dreadful incident necessitated replacement of the radar equipment. When the new equipment was installed, the whole thing had to be realigned in relation to various points of bearing in the surrounding landscape. A more senior officer than I came on site to carry out this alignment with a kinetheodolyte. It was a very complex business and outside my experience. I remember feeling that I still had a lot to learn.

Today, people's idea of the Home Guard is coloured by television's portrayal of Captain Mainwaring and Dad's Army. In fact, our home-grown Hampstead variety was a very different kettle-of-fish. There was a detachment on Hampstead Heath, adjacent to the gun site, of about sixty individually manned projectiles. These were designed to be fired simultaneously, but each at a slightly different angle, so that the pattern of explosions in the sky was spread over quite a large area. This Z battery got its information from the radar on E22.

I shall never forget the first time I heard them fire. The radar operators and I were in the radar cabin of the Mark II. Suddenly there was the most terrifying noise — ear shattering, whooshing, cracking noise and we all automatically ducked; though if it had been some horrifying new weapon coming down I doubt if ducking would have done us any good. After the target we were firing at had gone out of range, the sergeant radar operator asked the Command Post, "What the devil was that?" We were intrigued to hear that it was the Home Guard rocket battery.

In September 2003, BBC television put on a programme about one of the worst London tragedies of the War. On the evening of the 3rd of March 1943 an air raid warning sounded in Bethnal Green. Londoners were used to warnings and made for the nearest shelters in an orderly fashion. Suddenly the crowd outside the Underground Station panicked. Men, women and children at the entrance started to push forward. Those on the escalator hurried but some fell. The crowd behind continued to surge forward and the impetus behind those people caused them to fall on top of those lower down. Pile upon pile of bodies accumulated at the bottom. When it was all over, one hundred and seventy people were dead and hundreds injured. I did wonder when I read about it why Londoners who were not prone to panic had done so in this spectacular way.

In 2003, BBC researchers began to question what had happened and they found the answer. In Victoria Park a Z battery (Home Guard rockets) had recently been set up. Plans were made to test the rockets and it was decided to sound the air raid sirens and alert all the local services. There were no enemy planes overhead and no bombs coming down. When the rockets in Victoria Park Z battery were fired, all hell broke loose and people in the streets panicked.

To return to memories of Hampstead gun site, John Duck the Home Guard Captain was a regular visitor in our officers' mess. He often dropped in for a drink and a chat and was always welcomed as a friend. Some time before D Day John stopped coming and we missed him. We did wonder why he no longer put in an appearance. Had we hurt his feelings in some way or what? Two or three months went by and there was John Duck again. We were delighted to see him, but he offered no explanation of his absence. Things being as they were in wartime, we asked no questions. Some time after D Day we got an explanation. John was a big contractor and he had been down on the south coast engaged in building the Mulberry Harbours in preparation for the D-Day landing.

One other Home Guard man has a place in my story. At Whetstone Park, a scientist, who I think might have been Bedford, was carrying out some research of his own which in no way interfered with our normal radar equipment. He was a private in the Home Guard. Frequently he would appear on site in order to work on his experiments. This eminent scientist would trot up to the command post to announce his presence to the Gun Position Officer as everyone had to do. "Good evening, Sir (or Ma'am)." (Salute). "May I work on my equipment, Sir?" At the end of his evening's work, he would dust his knees, trot back to the command post, come to attention smartly. "Thank you very much, Sir!" — and off he would go, presumably to study intricate scientific recordings, with a view to improving London's defences.

For people serving in "operational commands in a theatre of war" the Air Minister had agreed that Ack-Ack Command was an operational command. The War Office said that the skies above Britain were a theatre of war but Ack-Ack personnel on the ground were not in the theatre. Sir Frederick Pile commented ironically that this idea was strange as military people in Ack-Ack Command had received honours such as the Military Medal, Military Cross and the DCM in the early days of the war. I think that people living in London and other heavily attacked areas being defended by our guns would have been surprised to be told that they were not in a theatre of war. Ack-Ack Command, in the years 1942 onwards, was responsible for the damage and destruction of more enemy planes than the Royal Air Force.

My poor radar mechanic on W14 who was killed by a bomb must have thought he was in a theatre of war.

CHAPTER
TWELVE

Life in the Mess

The Officers' Mess for E22 was a requisitioned house on the opposite side of the road from the gun site, at the Golders Green end of Hampstead Way. It was a typical red-brick suburban house on the corner of a side road, pleasant enough and commodious enough.

The ATS officers slept in the attic which, together with its bathroom, extended over the whole length of the house. Rosemary, the Junior Commander (three pips) slept on the first floor. As three of us shared one bedroom I felt quite at home. It was just like middle school years at my public school. I do not think there was anything on the floor in the way of carpeting; but we had some extremely pretty covers on our beds. They were patchwork quilts made by hand by Canadian women of the Red Cross. I remember them arriving and how a bit of colour lifted our spirits. "Thank you, Red Cross."

Colour was the thing that was missing in our lives. Nearly everything was khaki and I rebelled in a small way by adopting the most brilliantly coloured socks I could find in the shops — scarlet, emerald green and garish yellow. During the day these were concealed by boots and green-blancoed gaiters, so they only emerged in the Mess off duty when I was wearing shoes. Neither the CO nor Rosemary objected to this unorthodox gear: but then, I am sure I was regarded as slightly eccentric, in any case, being REME.

During working hours I had to be unorthodox anyway, as there were navy blue REME shoulder-flashes on my battle dress — a necessity — and incidentally navy-backed pips, of which I was very proud. We all wore the AA scarlet square on our sleeves — scarlet with a black bow and arrow. At a party in the evenings, if I ever managed to get to one, I wore my FANY uniform. Our Battery Commander, Arthur Gough, wore his London Scottish uniform, with grey trousers. I remember going to a party at Hyde Park and picking out a FANY uniform there. "Ben" Lodge had been in the 6th Western Motor Company with me in Chester.

With our battle dress, when we wore it on the gun site, in cold weather we wore leather jerkins and white suede mittens with an attached flap which buttoned over, when we did not need to use our fingers. Unfortunately we did need to use our fingers for the greater part of the time, so I remember suffering greatly with chilblains. We all, of course, wore the A.A. Command sign on our sleeves. It was a large scarlet square, with a black bow and arrow on it. Whoever designed it, I felt, had a somewhat cynical attitude to our work! We were not the bowmen of England — nor the Army's toxophilists. Churchill said in a 1954 speech: "It was the nation . . . that had the lion's heart.

124

I had the luck to be called upon to give the roar." In Ack-Ack we had the luck to be able to give a roar supplementary to Winston's: we were more noisy than the archers at Agincourt.

Christian names were, of course, the norm in the Mess, with the exception of the CO who was always "Sir". The charming Royal Artillery captain "Alex" was never about a great deal in the Mess off duty. I reckon his wife must have been nearby. He had an unusual mode of address. All the male officers were "Ned" and all the girls were "Nell".

It is hard to believe how small monthly Mess bills were. I have a copy of one for £2.10s. There was only a very limited amount of alcohol available in the Mess. I do remember that the Brigadier from 26 Brigade up the road seemed to have a sixth sense about when our small ration of whisky arrived. He always "dropped in" for a chat that evening. Gin did not suit me though, being young and inexperienced, I had not yet realised it. When we had a party I always drank gin and lime. It was not possible to drink a great deal — there was a case for FHB (family hold back) but I always wondered why, having started out quite looking forward to the evening, I gradually felt more and more gloomy as the evening went on and had difficulty in keeping up an appearance of jollity. Gin has a depressive effect on some people and I am one of them.

As in all parts of the services during the war, we had our infantile battles in the Mess. I remember one with fighting up and down the stairs, letting off fire-extinguishers with foam everywhere. I can recall another fight in which I was very much involved. I was accused of being "cheeky" and was carried by three male officers bodily out into the garden after lunch and dumped in the bird-bath. It was all done with great goodwill, but I do remember being really peeved because my dignity was injured and my trousers were sopping wet.

There were certain routines in the mess. One was to listen to the 6 o'clock and/or 9 o'clock news. Another was to listen to ITMA. It was always a great disappointment if we ever had to miss that. Of course there was only one "wireless" in the Mess, so we all gathered together to listen. It was a social occasion. We loved Colonel Chinstrap — "Water! What's that?" And I can still hear the voice of Mrs Mop — "Can I do you now, sir?"

Shortly after the war, I was walking up the Finchley Road from John Barnes in Hampstead. As I came to the L.M.S. Railway Station, a crowd was gathering on the pavement, near a coal depot which used to be there. I asked a lady in a mink coat what was happening. "Don't you know? We are all waiting for the hearse to go by. Tommy Handley is being cremated at Golders Green." At that moment a coalman came up from the Depot in full regalia, leather jerkin, denim trousers and shirt covered in coal dust, black face and cap. He joined the lady in the mink coat and they stood companionably together until the funeral procession had passed by. I thought how that scene was representative of the audience ITMA had had. People from every class of society enjoyed it and would not miss it for anything. Tommy was truly mourned.

When the V1s started coming over in large numbers, Arthur Gough our CO was worried about the women sleeping in our spacious attic. He had our mattresses brought down and stored in a cupboard in the hall. Each night we had to wait until the anti-room was clear, before we could install ourselves in there to sleep. When there was a Mess party, it was pretty late before we could settle down. Waking in the morning and inhaling stale cigarette smoke and the smell of beer was an unpleasant experience. One of the ATS officers brought her very large and slobbery dog to live in the Mess for a while. All dogs seemed to know the difference between the noise of RAF planes and V1s. This dog did and he panicked when he heard a V1 close to. He never went to his mistress's mattress, but always to mine. I found myself having to share a very slobbery pillow (and the rest of my mattress) with this large and heavy animal.

Talking of drinks, one summer evening the Major announced that it was his birthday and he invited any of the officers who were free to join him on a pub crawl. We walked up Hampstead Way and started at The Spaniards. It was a beautiful hot sunny evening. We just had an odd pint or so there and then went on to the Bull and Bush, where there was a gorgeous parrot which I always went to talk to, although everyone else said it did not exist. After a pinta at The Bull and Bush we strolled on to Jack Straw's Castle. I forget which was our fourth port of call. During the whole evening, we probably only had about three pints of watery beer! After that the little party returned to the mess.

In the morning I realised that my leather shoulder bag was missing. I had just become aware of it, when the telephone rang and it was someone from Hampstead Police Station. He asked whether we had a Subaltern Inkster in the mess. I went to speak to him and he said he had identified the owner of the bag by my chequebook. Would I please go down to Hampstead Police Station to collect it. At the next opportunity I did just that and the policeman behind the desk very formally asked me to tell him what were the contents of my bag. I enumerated several things including my cigarette case which was quite distinctive. He then grinned at me and said, "Where did you leave it?" I took a deep breath and said, "It might have been The Spaniards, it might have been The Bull and Bush, it might have been Jack Straw's Castle". He thought this was a huge joke and said, "You had quite a night of it, hadn't you!" What I should have replied was, "I do two miles to the gallon."

Some of the young, today, seem to think that officers were terribly spoilt because we had batmen (or women) to look after us. All they did was keep our living accommodation clean, look after our uniforms and generally help us in any way we needed. We *did* need! We all had almost non-stop jobs and would have been hard pushed to do what they did for us. My driver was also my batman — or woman — which ever I had at the time. Sometimes, if we had been away from Hampstead for a long time, one of the other batting people would take over my things good-naturedly. I think they all rather enjoyed working in the mess — a more "cushy" job than many others.

The only time I had to complain about a batman was when one of them, not mine, went AWOL, taking my lovely brass shell-case with him. I had been looking out for one and had had it specially burnished in Park Royal Workshop. This was shortly before the gun site ceased to function and I never seemed to have an opportunity to acquire another.

Christmas Day was as busy as any day in the year, for the inhabitants of the Officers Mess, I never remember alarm bells ringing on that day, but we were all up at crack of dawn, or before dawn cracked. All the women officers had to take early morning tea round to the male other-ranks and the male officers took tea round to the ATS. The gunners and REME men's reactions to being presented with a cuppa by a woman officer were very funny! At first they looked bashful, then they looked pleased and amused. Almost straight away we had to begin preparations for midday Christmas Dinner. The CO and Alex the captain carved turkeys when the time came and all the other officers served up the meal. We washed up afterwards, too. All this meant, of course, that we had no opportunity to have a Christmas Dinner ourselves. So we had our Christmas on Boxing Day.

There is a sequel to this Christmas story. Just as we were finishing the washing up after Christmas dinner a small crisis developed. A message came through that the radar needed to be on standby at 4 o'clock (known as "last light"). We were not given a clear-cut reason for this, but we needed to obey orders and all REME personnel were called out. We immediately made an extraordinary and disturbing discovery. The weather was very unusually cold. There had been snow, a slight thaw, a hard frost, more snow, slight thaw and another hard frost. The large and heavy turntable on which the radar receiver rotated had frozen solid. The mechanics switched on everything in the cabin, to get heat from above and, we hoped, heat penetrating down through the slip-rings. Blow-lamps were applied right round the outside and oil had to be heated and poured round the outside. All this took two or three hours and it was extremely lucky that this phenomenon had not occurred when a raid was expected.

CHAPTER
THIRTEEN

The Mind of a Radar Officer

When I cast my mind back to 1943 at E22 Hampstead, I think of myself sitting by an open fire in the ante-room of the Mess, reading a thin red book. I had picked up Sir James Jeans' "Physics and Philosophy" in the Charing Cross Road. I had often been working all the previous evening and a good part of the night, so I tried to snatch an hour or two off work in the afternoon, when other officers were working. It was quiet and cosy and I could concentrate on my reading. It was, for me, a pretty mind-stretching book, but not nearly so daunting as the volume on calculus which I had tried to study at Petersham. A whole new world was being opened to me which I explored in later years.

In my precious book, the quantum theory was explained and the new quantum theory in some detail. What I recall most vividly was the exploration of the borderlines between matter and energy waves. It made me ponder over the relationship between mind and matter. When later in life I worked in psychotherapy I was very receptive to discussion about the power of

131

mind over the human body and its parts. This linked up with my later study of theology and striving to understand the relationship between God and Man. Reinhold Niebuhr, the great protestant theologian, said: "The true Christ is not expected, because all human wisdom seeks to complete itself from the basis of its partial perspective." That is why I have always disliked saying the Creed, as they seem to be trying to "pin God down". I have always striven to make *my* perspective less partial.

Joyce Grenfell in "A letter to a Goddaughter" wrote, "I would wish for anybody I loved the possibility of never coming to the end of discovery." I have felt that in my life I have never come to the end of discovery. It has been a great joy to explore a little of the sciences and literature and the arts. I have always been filled with wonder about the nature of man and its possibilities.

Science has advanced since the end of the war in ways which would have been beyond my wildest dreams in 1943. But Aldous Huxley in "Ends and Means" made a wise comment: "Without progress in charity, technicological advance is useless. Indeed, it is worse than useless. Technical progress has merely provided us with more efficient means for going backward." These are all serious thoughts. What I have been trying to convey is the conviction that often one's whole life is influenced by things that happen quite early on. Future developments are there in embryo. So it was with me at Easy 22.

I bought "Physics and Philosophy" in the Charing Cross Road; there were wonderful book shops during the war. Their shelves were stuffed with beautiful leather-bound books, many first editions and marvellously illustrated volumes all going for a shilling or half a crown. An association of ideas made me think of "84 Charing Cross Road" — that dearly-loved book. That made me think of Leo Marks, the son of the owner of number 84. Leo was a brilliant leading light in the organisation of coding in Baker Street during the war and wrote that extraordinary book "Between Silk and Cyanide", describing his contacts with men and women dropped by parachute into France and Holland. He employed several FANYs in coding and decoding. I remember my sister Brenda, a FANY, when she came up to London for a night from Bletchley Park, taking me to Baker Street and going in to consult with someone. I was ignominiously left outside and not given any clue about her business. I retaliated to some extent that night by laying on an air raid for Brenda. The Overseas Club, of which I was a member, had parked us out in The Duke of York's Chambers in Duke of York Street. During the raid, Hyde Park gun site opened up; Brenda did not like the noise much.

Now I come to think of it, another sisterly memory was of her telephone calls to me. I would just have gone to bed after an exhausting day. "Marjorie! Telephone call for you." Down I trundled to the hall where there was the only telephone in the Mess. It was my sister, bright and breezy, just about to go on night shift at Bletchley. "Just thought I'd ring you to see how you are." Being the elder by nearly four years, she did tend to boss me about still and she was certainly more sophisticated.

At the age of 20–21 I was very inexperienced and naïve about sexual matters. In this, I was not at all unusual in those days. I had learned how to conduct myself from Presbyterian parents who were at the same time very warm, caring, affectionate people. Their own marriage was very sound. A good marriage of parents can cause problems in their children. I remember discussing this with a younger university friend who had the same problem. It is difficult to find a partner for life who would match up to the high standards set by one's parents.

I was fairly strongly attracted to men, without, I think, any bi-sexual tendencies: but I had an attitude, I think caught from my sister, that one should not "encourage" a man: that he should do all the chasing. I literally *did not know* how to flirt. This was so, in spite of the fact that a boyfriend early in the war told me that I had "come-to-bed-eyes". This probably made me a little anxious. I was a very romantic little thing, however. Once it was very serious indeed: but fortune has its part to play in these things.

Having lost my home and possessions early in 1941, I was in a peculiar position. I had no home, as most of my friends had, in which I could dump my belongings or retrieve them as and when I wanted them. Indeed I had no possessions. I had no gramophone or records, no camera, no tennis racquet or balls, no civilian clothes worth mentioning — at least no evening dress or evening shoes. I had no documents from my previous life and I even had to obtain copies of my birth certificate and school certificates in order to go to OCTU. I had been stripped in a flash of all jewellery and all childhood books and toys. Everything I did possess had to come with me. I learnt to live a very spartan existence, though of course I did not suffer the terrible conditions endured by men in battle on sea and land and in the air.

One beautiful possession I did allow myself soon after reaching Hampstead. On my first day off, I strolled down Hampstead High Street and looked in the window of a junk shop. There I saw a beautiful pair of porcelain figures and thought I would go in to ask the price. They were extremely grubby, but as far as I could see they were completely intact. When I asked the price, however, I was horrified! They cost 14 guineas!! I said regretfully, no I could not afford them. At the time I was being paid about £10 a month. Unfortunately I could not forget these figures, so a month later I went back to have another look. They were still there. This time I had saved a little money and succumbed to the temptation. And they survived through all air raids on my bedside table. When they gave me the bill, they wrote on the bottom "Two French Figures". About five years ago I took them to an antiques road show and David Battie looked at them. I produced the bill but he had already identified them as German and I said, "Yes, I thought they were German, although the bill said they were French." He grinned and said, "How unpatriotic of you."

Although I did not begin to acquire many antiques until many years after the war, partly because I had no home of my own, I did eventually acquire some beautiful things, handed down from my parents. Two lovely porcelain pictures of Japanese palaces are among my treasured possessions. Their history is most romantic. My father, Robert Inkster, had an uncle Robert who traded in the Far East in the mid-to-late nineteenth century. He fell in love with a Shogun lady, whose family considered themselves semi-royal and would never have consented to her marrying Robert. The couple eloped to Singapore and settled there. She brought from Japan these two porcelain pictures. Robert and she had no children and she died fairly young. Robert lived there until he died and bequeathed the pictures to his sister, Catherine. Aunt Kitty, my great aunt, settled with her husband, a retired sea-captain, about a mile from our home in Cheshire. Our family were all fond of her and visited frequently. When she died, she left the pictures to her nephew, my father.

Our delightful Presbyterian minister had been very fond of these beautiful things, so my father generously lent him one. When our house was bombed, the other one of the pair was on the wall in our drawing room. Although only one wall of that room was left intact, amazingly, two pictures on it were comparatively unscathed. The lacquer frame of the Japanese one was slightly cracked and chipped, but the porcelain unharmed. The other, with our minister, went up to Cumbria when he retired and came back to us when he was a very old man. The history of the journeyings of these two beautiful, very vulnerable objects is most romantic: from Japan to Singapore: from there to Aunt Kitty on the Wirral peninsula: from her home to my father's home, one up to Cumbria and back, both into store during the war, after surviving the bombing of my home: from there to two addresses in Hampstead: to my sister's home in Hammersmith: to Epsom: to Rickmansworth: and finally to my home near Oxford.

During the war, men in combat, on invasion beaches, or in desert, or in any other unspeakable conditions of warfare, were deprived of just about everything, even often of life itself; but certainly of everything beautiful, man-made or natural. To be stripped of so much, as so many people, including civilians, found, was an experience which brought them up against the reality of self. Even in the midst of fear of danger, life became curiously simple. Material things were no longer of great importance. In my comparative safety and comparative comfort I developed a curiously puritanical streak and it was not until about 20 years or so after the war that I recovered a wish to buy furniture or porcelain or pictures. Possessions remain of relatively little importance. Pre-war generations generally felt differently, though my parents, who lost nearly everything when my home was bombed, were wonderfully courageous about all that. To them relationships were all important.

CHAPTER
FOURTEEN

Life Outside Camp

I mentioned joining my parents in Aberdeen between my two periods of radar training — New Year in 1941–42. The train journey from London was pretty grim. Corridors of trains were always packed on these long-distance journeys. I spent the first three or four hours sitting on my suitcase. Going to the lavatory was a major exercise, stumbling over other peoples' luggage or trampling on their feet and legs. There were, of course, no lights, so everything had to be done by a process of feeling! Then I had a stroke of luck. Someone in the compartment I was standing or sitting next to got up to leave the train. I nipped into his seat and found myself surrounded by Polish air force characters. They were going up to Perth. I had a most entertaining journey, but as we got within half an hour of Perth, things got a little embarrassing. At first I thought it was just a joke when the airman sitting next to me said he thought I ought to get off at Perth with him! As time went on, I discovered that he was serious, though drunk, and quite determined. I needed to be rescued by his friends who convinced him that his plans for me were unrealistic. I heaved a great sigh of relief when the train finally arrived at Perth and they seized him by both arms and hauled him off. It was New Year's Eve and they had been celebrating — though not too objectionably. I do remember arriving at Aberdeen some time later, in the early hours, just as it was getting light. As I left the station I encountered a dense fog and was entertained by dim figures who had been celebrating and were staggering through the gloom. I suppose I must have found a taxi or an early bus in order to avoid them.

Shorter train journeys during the war could be tricky, especially if one wanted to get out at a small station in a string of small stations. Platforms were very dimly lit and the names of the villages and towns were in small letters under shaded lights. Some of the trains were decidedly ancient. Once, when travelling down to a village in Essex to stay with friends, I was amazed to find at Liverpool Street that the train was lit by gas.

Getting on and off underground trains in Central London latish in the evening could be hazardous. Many Londoners had taken to sleeping on the platforms and their sleeping mattresses or bunks took up about half the platform width. The smell of inadequately-washed humanity was pretty powerful and nauseating. A good proportion of sleepers had been bombed out of their homes, so washing of clothes or of themselves was appallingly difficult. The whole scene on the platform was quite bizarre and has been depicted by Government-appointed war artists.

If you were unlucky enough to be south of the river in the train when an air raid warning went, it was just too bad, because no trains were allowed to run under the Thames during a raid. So you just had to wait.

Glamour on evenings out was restricted by regulations about when we could wear civilian clothes. My father had a cousin, George Robertson, who was secretary for agriculture in Northern Ireland and used to have to come over to London fairly often. He generously used to invite me out for the evening, but I was in uniform. This meant carrying my respirator and tin hat. There was no suitable dumping-ground for these at the Hungaria Restaurant, so they had to go with me to the table. We danced on a pocket-handkerchief sized dance floor. George, bless his heart, kindly brought me a present each time he came to London. It was always a packet of expensive cigarettes — either Balkan Sobranie or Black Russian, which made me feel very sophisticated because they were black with gold tips. It was thanks to George that I stopped smoking after the war. I had acquired expensive taste in cigarettes, could no longer stomach cheaper brands. On an ex-Service grant, I could not afford Sobranies or Black Russian: so I gave up smoking.

Just after Christmas time in 1944 the other radar maintenance officers in north London decided to give Marjorie a treat. I was told to arrange a day off for myself and four of my RMO colleagues collected me. They took me out to lunch and then — guess what — the great treat was revealed. We were going to the Windmill Theatre ("We never closed") to see Phyllis Dixie!! I do not imagine the RMOs thought that I would be thrilled by the sight of naked female figures. It was more of a treat for them!! But the matinee programme had a variety of "acts" apart from Phyllis Dixie and was thoroughly enjoyable. The Phyllis Dixie part was in tableau form. Naked women were not allowed to be seen moving in those days, but as far as I can remember the scenes were very artistically done. I think my REME colleagues were salving their consciences that day, because although I was trained at Petersham with men and doing exactly the same job as they were, I was being paid about two thirds as much as they were.

The pay situation was the fault of the ATS, not REME. My REME major did his best for me. When he discovered that I was receiving pay which was less than my own staff sergeants, the major moved heaven and earth to arrange that I should receive REME corps pay which certainly made the difference of a few pounds per month. As I have remarked earlier, the ATS "bigwigs" seemed determined to forget the existence of women radar mechanics and RMOs. A book containing descriptions of ATS trades and trade tests, issued in 1943, contains descriptions of tests for the radar operators working on mixed gun sites, but makes no mention at all of radar mechanics.

To return to extra-mural activities. I did occasionally have a chance to enjoy something more exciting than Phyllis Dixie. I remember two parties at the Savoy. I was taken dancing at the Berkley, dancing to one of the famous dance bands. Another time there was a box at the theatre in a party of four, followed by night-clubbing. The clubbing started at the Astor. After a lot of dancing, we decided to move on to the Coconut Grove in Regent Street. I took off my shoes to cool my feet and walked through Leicester Square and Piccadilly in stockinged feet. At the Coconut Grove, it was incredibly dark — good for dancing cheek to cheek. After a while a new bottle of gin was delivered to our table and I must have been the first to take some of it. In no time at all, I felt ill and sick. It was poison! The Coconut Grove, we discovered later, was renowned for serving "bad" gin. That was the end of the evening: my partner delivered me back to E22 in a taxi and I got myself to bed and to sleep. Oh boy, did I feel awful in the morning! This was the one and only hangover I have ever had as I am gifted with an incredibly strong head for alcohol and I suppose I have always been extremely careful about drinking ever since that night.

After my home was destroyed by a bomb, my mother was in a nursing home in Heswall for three weeks. Then my father and she stayed in a country pub up the River Dee, near the Iron Bridge, Chester for about a month. Brenda, my sister, was unexpectedly posted to Wolverhampton, driving for the Royal Dutch Army. Their CO had written to the FANY Commanding Officer asking for Brenda to be posted with them as their ambulance driver, because they needed her "in case of bombardment". I remained in Chester until my radar training began in September 1941, so I was able to see a good deal of my parents. By September, when I was sent to London for training, they had gone north to my father's home city, Aberdeen. The Inkster family house was up in the Scottish Deeside and two unmarried aunts were living there still. My mother was slowly recovering from her injuries and her health was very fragile. That winter of 1941 was one of the worst Scotland had seen for some time and she suffered greatly from the cold. I travelled north after Christmas for a short leave, between my two radar courses, and was almost snowed up when I was due to return south.

For the next two or three years, my annual leave periods and often 48 hour leave periods were spent with my parents. Having shared with them the dangers of being bombed and buried alive, I felt our relationship was very precious. I turned down other invitations in order to spend my time with them. I was glad when, having endured one gruelling winter in the north of Scotland, they came south and settled in a private hotel in the centre of Oxford. By that time I was stationed in London so I got to know Paddington Station well.

During one of my 48-hour leave periods in Oxford, victory came to us at El Alamein. The Government gave permission for bells to be rung. They had been silenced ever since the threat of invasion in 1940. I could not have chosen a better place to be than Oxford. Just imagine what it was like! Every bell rang, from Great Tom of Christchurch to the littlest bell in the suburbs. It warmed our hearts and filled us with new hope.

My brother Fraser was a fighter pilot and Brenda was by 1942 at Bletchley Park. It did not occur to me for some time, but our parents must have found things difficult, because none of the three of us could talk about our jobs at all. Lack of information about what we were doing must have been most frustrating. I was annoyed not to be able to share our everyday jokes on the gun site with them. Nor did it occur to me that my mother was afraid I might get killed during what was called the "Little Blitz".

Fraser was almost a worse letter-writer than I was, so I more or less lost touch with him until after VE Day, when he was CO at Clifton, York. On a visit to him there I learnt to play Liar Dice. When I returned to my London mess I discovered I was such a good liar that I could often win enough money to pay my fare from Paddington to Oxford.

Fraser, with a small chorus of officers, taught me an "enactment" which I had not heard before.

Leader: "They're pulling down our old pub"
Chorus: "Boo!"
Leader: "They're building another one"
Chorus: "Hurray!"
"Only one bar"
"Boo!"
"Thirty yards long"
"Hurray!"
"Only one barman"
"Boo!"
"Fifty barmaids"
"Hurray!" and so on, as you like. He also taught me two "shaggy dog" stories, a pattern very common at that time.

144

I saw a little more of Brenda who came to stay in the mess at Hampstead more than once. I was able to show her over the radar and I went to Bletchley Park twice because I was security-cleared. Bletchley was never bombed, because its secrets were so well kept that the Germans never knew about it. Churchill spoke of Bletchley as "the goose that laid the golden egg but never cackled". The only time Brenda experienced bombing was one night when we met in London and stayed the night in Duke of York Street, near the Hyde Park gun site. That was a noisy night.

Meanwhile my father was doing something rather special in the way of war work. It is quite a long story and I need to go back in time to the pre-war days 1936-39. Brenda left school before she was 17 and went out to Germany to live with a very charming German family in Hanover. Frau von Reden treated her like a daughter and Brenda went riding and swimming and was taken to luxurious balls. She spent a few months at Heidelberg University and by 1939 spoke German almost like a native. She came home for a month or two during the summer of 1938 and brought with her Harald, one of the von Reden sons, to spend some time with our family in Cheshire.

Harald turned out to be an out and out Nazi — unlike the rest of his family. He behaved meticulously politely to us and did not talk too much about his beliefs, except to chunter on endlessly about how dangerous the Jews and the Communists were. He was 19 at the time and seemed keen to go exploring on his own, with a particular interest in Liverpool. We thought he seemed to spend an inordinate amount of time on the overhead railway there. A good bit of the overhead line ran over the docks, which were extensive.

When war broke out, Harald joined the German air force and became a bomber pilot. At one stage he was bombing Liverpool and he may even have dropped the bomb which hit our home? Quite early on in the war he was shot down by Ack-Ack. Surviving comparatively uninjured, he was sent as a POW to an officers' camp at Swanwick in Derbyshire. The prisoners were given the chance to write to one chosen person in Britain and he opted to write to my father, who had impressed him. My father said he would be interested to write to him; and so began a correspondence which continued throughout the war.

The picture that emerged was of a very enlightened regime at Swanwick. Our young Nazi described talks and discussions; opportunities to vent feelings about everything and everyone the prisoners hated; examination of the history of Nazism and learning about our British attitudes. Almost imperceptibly at first, the young bomber pilot's attitude changed and it became increasingly obvious in his letters. My father was an elder of the Presbyterian Church, with strong beliefs, but sensitive and never dogmatic. He must have helped in the process of change. About four years after the war, when he was studying law, Harald came to Britain and visited my parents. He described his change of attitude and said how much he owed to my father's correspondence and other experiences he had during the war.

I would like to indulge in a little nostalgia. At the beginning of the war, when I was still at home, travelling into Liverpool daily for my secretarial course, my mother and I shared the task of dealing with all the windows in the house. The authorities were aware of what terrible injuries could be inflicted by broken glass. All households were advised to buy reels of a special sticky tape and put strips of it in a cross-cross pattern diagonally across all our windows. As ours was a three storey house with fourteen rooms and large windows this was quite a task. It did not occur to us at the time that this was not going to be particularly effective when a 1,000 lb bomb fell directly on our home.

Another recollection of days early in the war is set in the intense heat of early summer 1940. It was the hottest summer I can remember. I had finished my secretarial course and was waiting for the FANY company in Chester to send me to Pinewood for initial training. I recall lazy afternoons basking in the sun, but shading my face with a Japanese sunshade made of waxed paper. The varnish had a very distinctive smell when in the hot sun. Every now and then there was a rather rattley sort of noise and what we called an "autogyro" passed over the garden. Occasionally a bi-plane meandered past. From that to the first jet plane was only four or five years: only fifty years later I looked up at the sky one night in Majorca and saw the spark of light of a spacecraft crossing the sky. I remember my father describing to me carriage and horses going down Regent Street, with footmen wearing powdered wigs standing at the back. He lived into his 90s to see the first men landing on the moon. As Matthew Arnold asked in his poem "The Forsaken Merman" — "Children dear, was it yesterday?"

While I am in this mood, recalling early days of the war, I remember curious little details about the bomb days. When I was dug out of the ruins, I had miraculously sustained no injuries except superficial scrapes on forehead and knees: but I was curiously deaf. When back with my FANY unit in Chester, my CO, Woodburn, insisted on a medical check-up and our medical officer found that my ears were full of plaster. I was dispatched to the Army Hospital to have my ears syringed. I can see so vividly the bright blue uniforms of all the patients who were out of bed. Surely they do not make them wear these today?! Then I remember the rather crude handling of the medical orderly, who appeared never to have syringed an ear before. The water he used was at first scaldingly hot until I shouted. Then he directed the flow of water onto my eardrum with such violence that the whole world revolved alarmingly around me. Later in life I learnt how tenderly ears should be treated. From 1943 onwards my ears were submitted to further ill-treatment at Primrose Hill and Mill Hill, when 5.25 guns fired.

To return to the plaster from my bombed house — it was thickly in my hair, giving me a grey, middle-aged appearance. I rushed to wash it away, but only partially succeeded. The plaster had a disgusting smell of decay which lingered in my hair for weeks, the smell being reawakened each time I

148

washed it, overcoming the scent of my Amami shampoo. This evokes the memory of a skit on a romantic love-song to an Ack-Ack girl: "I love the scent of cordite in your hair!"

CHAPTER
FIFTEEN

V1 and V2

On 15th June 1944 we encountered the first V1. A few experimental launchings had occurred on 13th June. Initial problems were more or less resolved on 14th June. On the 15th, 444 bombs were launched. Many fell into the sea but 60% reached English soil. 73 reached Greater London. At Hampstead we had had the usual alarm bells and all the equipment was manned. I took myself to the Mark II receiver and we picked up our first target. At that moment I had no inkling that anything untoward was happening. The signal on the range cathode-ray tube looked worryingly small to me. Could there be something wrong with our radar? The height at which the thing was coming in was extraordinarily low. A message came through from Stanmore, "Diver, diver, diver." We were, of course, aware that we had to expect new weapons. I have to confess that my memory of what happened next is distinctly hazy. I seem to remember that the battery commander had to go to his safe in the battery office to find a sealed order which gave him much information about "Diver" which was the V1. It soon became apparent that gun sites in built-up areas could not continue to fire at these machines. Because they flew so low we were in danger of shooting people's chimneys off. In any case there was little point in shooting them down in the midst of streets and houses where they would explode. We ceased to fire at them.

This was all very frustrating. Sometimes in the early evening we would stroll across Hampstead Heath and stand on the high ground, gazing at the V1s at they came in with their blazing tails rather like illuminated feathers, and their curious, throaty noise, like a sewing machine with a bad cold. The sky was seldom free of them. When the engine cut out, there was a pause before they hit the ground. If one was indoors and could not see them, one suffered a certain degree of apprehension about divers which were not actually overhead and therefore not a direct threat to one's own safety. Some took much longer to glide to earth than others. Somehow, being threatened by these things was much worse than being threatened by a piloted plane. There was something creepy about it all.

On 15th June, 73 bombs reached Greater London causing much destruction and many deaths. Each contained 1,870 lbs of high explosive. In the 16 days following, over 2,440 flying bombs were launched: about 800 reached Greater London causing 2,441 deaths and many more serious injuries. On 18th June one landed on the Guards' Chapel during the service and 121 people were killed. This was for the Germans a lucky hit, because their bombardment by its very nature was indiscriminate. The V1 was not aimed at military targets but generally over a wide area at the civilian population. The launchings continued through July and August. On 2nd August, in 24 hours 108 missiles exploded in the London area.

When the V1s started to come over, they created many peculiar situations. One summer evening, while it was still light, I was in an underground train returning to Golders Green, which was the nearest station to Hampstead gun site. We emerged from the underground tunnel soon after leaving the Hampstead station. Immediately we could hear the strange chuntering noise of the V1 nearly overhead. The engine cut out and with one accord all the passengers sensibly got down on the floor. We were trapped in a tube of glass and glass could be a killer. But there remained one solitary figure hanging on to an overhead strap. It was a Major who looked disdainfully down at the rest of us. Luckily for him, the V1 did not land near enough to break any of the windows. He thought we were all cowards. The passengers all thought we were sensible.

I had one equally near-squeak from a V1, when in my utility truck going over to Whetstone Park at midday: there was a shopping street on the Finchley Road, with an unusually busy amount of traffic and people on the pavements. I was deep in my notebook, checking what needed to be looked at on the next gun site. The noise of our own engine and surrounding traffic smothered the noise of an approaching V1. Suddenly there was an almighty crash close to — but luckily for us not too near. I said, "Wow" to my driver. "That was quite near, wasn't it?" "Yes, ma'am," said my imperturbable driver, "I thought there must be something about. I noticed that everyone round us was lying down on the pavement." "Well, you might have warned *me*," I said rather indignantly.

During this whole period, of course, there were two ways in which the British were attempting to defend against the "doodlebugs" as they were nicknamed. The launching-sites had been identified quite early and were heavily bombed, but they were wide-spread and cleverly hidden. Many of the more experienced mixed anti-aircraft batteries were fairly soon moved out of London into the open country near the south coast. There were in fact two or three moves for strategic purposes. The Royal Air Force devised various methods of causing the V2s to crash, often into the English Channel. Meanwhile, the allies landed in Normandy on 6th June.

On 1st September the last of 8,617 flying bombs was launched in Northern France. During early September Heinkels were used to carry and launch V1s from Holland and Beauvais in France — about 300–400 more V1s — some of the Heinkels attacking by flying up the Thames estuary. 77 Heinkels were lost during the whole operation. In total, 7,488 crossed the coast: nearly 4,000 shot down before reaching targets. Deaths numbered just over 6,000, with nearly 18,000 people injured. It is known that during a good part of the time the doodlebugs were flying, many failed to function properly, blowing up on the launching pad, falling to earth on French soil or diving into the sea. I think something like two thirds of the original launching pads were destroyed by our bombers before the first launchings. Large numbers of V1s were shot into the sea by RAF fighters or tipped in, with the fighters' wing tips. Large numbers were eventually shot down by anti-aircraft. The proportion of AA kills crept up until at the end it was an almost unbelievable 80%.

Had none of these things happened — had the Germans succeeded in launching most of the V1s before we could begin Overlord — the numbers of V1s reaching London would have been horrific. The amount of death and destruction there would have been in our capital does not bear thinking about. The planning of these robots, to be aimed at the general civilian population, must have started early in the war. Yet the Germans screamed with horror at the doings of Bomber Harris towards the end of hostilities.

Although it was impossible to shoot at V1s in London, their advent affected me personally very much indeed. My much-loved battery, 476, was picked out as one of the units to be moved out of London. When the major told us, he turned to me and said, "Of course, we are taking you too, Marjorie!" I was delighted. Sadly, however, it transpired that the radar they were to use was the American 584 — admittedly better even than our Canadian Mark III. I had not yet been trained in its use and there was no time for me to do the course. When everyone except me packed up and drove away on that sad morning, I felt utterly bereft. The radar mechanics and NCOs were, of course, still on the gun site but I was to be deserted in the Mess, until the replacement battery from Scotland arrived later that day. I must indeed have looked "bereft" as 476 officers prepared to leave. Our dear Alex (Captain Alexander) took one look at me and wrote out a BLR certificate to give to me addressed to Nell. I have it still: but I always was a sentimental old so and so! BLR stands for Beyond Local Repair and was used when items of equipment were worn out or unusable and had to be returned to the Quartermaster's stores.

Incidentally, although I cannot remember 476's immediate destination in November 1944, the battery ended up in Belgium, defending Antwerp against V1s. Major Millington describes how they went into action on Christmas Day and by the end of January had shot down 19 V1s. Colin Dobinson, in his excellent book "AA Command" in the chapter "Monuments to compromise" page 457 says, "AA guns on the continent destroyed 2,356 flying bombs which the Germans had been targeting on Belgium." ... "Many of the gunners serving on the continent had actually been trained by Ack-Ack Command — this is where many of Pile's better men had gone." His sources evidently did not show that it was actually whole mixed heavy ack ack batteries, girls and all, which had been transferred, as 476 was from London to Belgium. I kept up with my friends in Belgium, where they seemed to be busy shooting down V1s but having a much more lively social life and I was quite envious. Some remained friends through peacetime days and for years afterwards.

The replacement battery at Hampstead was a shower. The CO was very different from Arthur Gough, whom I liked and respected so much. The new CO was the only man in war time whom I could accuse of sexual harassment. Whenever he managed to sit next to me, he pinched my thighs in a really aggressive way. I made my feelings quite clear. The whole battery was sloppy and inefficient, in dress, in procedures and training. I do not believe they even bothered to check dials, as 476 had done without fail each day. I was quite alarmed by their slackness and made my feelings known in the REME workshops in no uncertain terms. I think the vibes in Anti-Aircraft Command worked quickly and efficiently. That battery was replaced in three weeks time. The replacement, to my relief, was much better and its members became my friends.

I have made no mention of the V2s, first launched on 8th September. By mid-October, the defences against V1s were well-established and that was a great relief. I found the V2s much easier to cope with emotionally, because there was none of the prolonged agony of wondering whether the V1 was going to cut its engine and land on *you*. With V2, there was just an almighty bang followed by the delayed rumble of the sound of its descent. You were either alive or you were not.

The V2 had a range of 150–200 miles, reached enormous heights of up to 50 miles and came down at about 1,800 miles an hour. From start to finish it took about five or six minutes. In March 1945 our gun sites in London were fitted with pyrotechnic launchers attached to the command post intended as warning of V2s, but as the V2 could not be fired on, there seemed little point in having a few minutes warning of their arrival, so those launchers were not used. At E22, ours were used on VE Day, set off by our naughty radar mechanics in celebration. I was in Oxford on leave that day so did not hear them, but apparently the prolonged howling noise was quite spectacular (or whatever the appropriate word is for noise)! I was sorry I missed it!

Luckily many of the V2s exploded in the clouds, before they reached earth. At night one could see this happen and hear it and one exploded in the air over our off-site W9. Everything seemed to happen at Willy-nine. The following morning, when I went over to them, one could see pieces of metal and plastic and rubber tubing strewn all over the grass and huts. It made me shudder to think what W9 would have been like if the V2 had actually landed on the gun site. Injuries, death and destruction would have been appalling.

One morning I was on the command post at Easy 22 talking to one of the spotters. She said, "You know, Ma'am, you can sometimes see the V2 going up." It was a cloudless morning and a few minutes later I could see what she meant. You did not actually see the rocket, which was, of course, far too far away, but you caught a glimpse of sunlight striking the cone and then could see the long trail of smoke from its exhaust as it climbed, apparently slowly, up into the sky. The spotter said, "Wait five minutes or so and we may hear it when it comes down." And so we did: an explosion in the distance luckily not near us.

In view of my choice of title for this book, I was amused to find that the code-name for the assault by German V-weapons was Crossbow.

Just before VE-Day in mid-April 1945 the British Army first entered Belsen. The sufferings of its inhabitants were exposed to the world for the first time in all their horror. Starvation and sickness had reduced these human beings to stinking skeletons. Many were unable to stand and many more died in the next two or three weeks in spite of all the help given to them by the troops rescuing them. I remember one of our REME corporals from Hampstead was among those soldiers. I imagine that volunteers were asked for, to take their turn in this harrowing task. He returned to us after a fairly short period — a matter of weeks — at a time when we were eagerly anticipating the end of the European war. Corporal Young was very subdued. I got him to act as my driver in order to keep him occupied. When I asked him whether he wanted to talk about what he had seen in Belsen, he said no. He did, however, describe the night before his unit entered the camp. The wind changed late in the evening and the stench from Belsen was nauseating. He spoke of this while driving through Golders Green in our utility truck. Suddenly he drew into the curb and got out. I wondered if he was going to be sick: but no. This sensitive man came back with a large bunch of daffodils and thrust them into my arms. There was no need to say anything. He needed the freshness and beauty and the scent to counteract memories of what he had experienced.

CHAPTER
SIXTEEN

Running down towards the End of War

As the war drew towards its end, Ack-Ack Command began to change rapidly. Many of the gun sites closed down. I was withdrawn to Park Royal Workshops and spent some time checking inventories. I hated this job: but quite shortly I escaped when I was Unit Education Officer for the first Ack-Ack Workshop Company REME and given my third pip.

The army had quite an enlightened attitude towards the servicemen who were awaiting discharge, from VE Day onwards. A great deal of effort was put into the problem of preventing them from getting bored. In some cases they were taking up the threads of studies which had been interrupted by wartime service. We were exceptionally lucky at Park Royal because a REME unit was composed of an unusually large number of intelligent men. Through distribution of questionnaires, we discovered a wealth of potential teachers and class leaders. Eventually 40 different classes and groups were running for 1,000 men. The ATS had their own classes. The REME had economics classes, beginners French, beginners German, advanced French, simple mathematics, advanced mathematics and so on.

To relieve the monotony, a request came through from the War Office for me to go and demonstrate various pieces of army electrical equipment, at an exhibition in Dorland Hall, Lower Regent Street. The exhibition was run by the Women's Electrical Association, which I was fascinated to learn had been founded by Caroline Hazlett, the woman engineer who had been consulted by Frederick Pile about the possibilities of women working in technical jobs on gun sites.

Of course, radar could not be put on display: so I had to go and get instruction on pieces of equipment I had never worked on. One, I remember, was a mine detector! I enjoyed myself for a week or two and met some very interesting people, including the Queen (later Queen Mum), the Prime Minister's wife, Lady Macmillan, and the really beautiful Duchess of Kent, with her crooked smile and delightful Greek accent. I have never had to talk so consistently nearly all day and was in danger of losing my voice a couple of times.

As the end of my service in REME drew to an end, one of the staff sergeants gave me an illustration of a kindness and helpfulness they had always shown me. One morning he said, "You're going up to the university, aren't you? I don't suppose you've got a wireless set, have you? But you'll need one." He said that if I could pay for the constituent parts, transformer, valves, etc, he would make a set for me in his spare time. And so he did. It was most beautifully finished in polished wood: nothing "home made" about it. The quality of the sound was superb. I used it for many years. He wanted nothing for his work: it was a free gift, a token of friendship. I could hardly believe such kindness.

CHAPTER
SEVENTEEN

End of War

Having just come away from watching the march past the Cenotaph on Remembrance Sunday, I sit down to write my last chapter. I was once more overwhelmed by the sheer numbers of courageous men and women who came to pay respect to the dead. It made me realise how small a thing Anti-Aircraft Command was in relation to the whole. Be assured that we were never unaware of what was going on in the outside world. The six o'clock and nine o'clock news were our main source of information — censored as they were. Our forces, invasion of Italy, El Alamein, D Day, naval battles, they were all part of the total picture which gave meaning to what we were doing.

After VE Day, I was withdrawn into workshops and everything in my work seemed an anti-climax. My new job was to be Education Officer for the REME Company and I got my third pip. I rather undeservedly was presented with a Certificate of Merit at a parade of the whole company. It was signed by General Pile, although in his book "A.A. Command" he never mentioned that there were women among his REME personnel.

So I took up my life as I should have done in 1939 and went up to the University.

I remember with gratitude a lively and affectionate childhood: a challenging war: demanding university years: inspiring years serving the church and in psychotherapeutic work: difficult years working with social workers. I have seen and heard and often shared some of other men and women's pain, though never suffered the appalling disasters so very many endure today. There have always been many great friendships and much good fortune. My life is a patchwork of happiness and sorrow, held together by an enduring Christian Faith.

O Joy! that in our embers
Is something that doth live,
That nature yet remembers
What was so fugitive!
The thought of our past years in me doth breed
Perpetual benediction.

Not for these I raise
The song of thanks and praise:
But for those obstinate questionings
Of sense and outward things,
Fallings from us, vanishings:
Blank misgivings of a creature
Moving about in worlds not realised,
High instincts before which our mortal nature
Did tremble like a guilty thing surprised:
But for those first affections,

Those shadowy recollections,
Which, be they what they may,
Are yet the fountain-light of all our day,
Are yet a master-light of all our seeing.

Our noisy years seem moments in the being
Of the eternal Silence: truths that wake
To perish never
Which neither listlessness nor mad endeavour
Nor man nor boy,
Nor all that is at enmity with joy,
Can utterly abolish or destroy.

Wordsworth. Ode. "Intimations of Immortality"

NOTES

FANY (First Aid Nursing Yeomanry)

The only women's yeomanry in the British Army. Founded shortly before the First World War, when many were nursing and in some cases organising and running field hospitals in France. During the Second World War the FANY were labelled Women's Transport Service and most FANY at first drove staff cars and ambulances. Quite early on, some were recruited into Intelligence, a good many worked in SOE and some were specially trained to work with the French resistance and dropped by parachute into France and Holland.

As the war progressed, FANYs infiltrated many spheres of army life. Some went to Bletchley Park, others went into AA Command and yet others into research on artillery sites in East Anglia. Pre-war, FANYs had had their own uniforms, made of beautiful barathea, but early on in the war they were dragooned into becoming part of the Auxiliary Territorial Service (ATS). Somehow they managed to retain their own identity as a service within a service. FANYs were never very military. FANY officers hated to be saluted and in the early days FANY "other ranks" would do almost anything to avoid having to salute ATS officers. FANY uniforms were kept for "special" occasions but FANYs in ATS uniform were allowed to wear special FANY flashes on their shoulders and to wear the straps of their uniform hats over the top of their heads.

INNER LONDON ARTILLERY ZONE

This zone was within a large, roughly oval area encompassing about 67 gun sites, north and south of the Thames. During the Blitz of 1941, this zone was grossly deficient in the sites which had been planned pre-war, and anti-aircraft was therefore inadequate to its task. In 1943 the number of sites had been greatly increased. In North London, the zones stretched quite a bit north of Hampstead. This was particularly important when German planes started coming in over the Wash, hoping by this means to avoid the heavily defended areas between the south coast and London.

FROM WAR OFFICE PUBLICATION ABOUT ATS

(Discovered very late in my writing of this book. Sent to me by REME Museum)

At first trained as radio mechanics for the RAOC, many women were employed from August 1941 onwards in trades which, on the formation of REME in October 1942, became known as REME Trades. Their training and trade tests were identical with those taken by the men they replaced and were designed to fit them for the operation, maintenance, repair, modification, inspection, installation and overhaul of army equipment particular to their trade. A certain number of ATS officers were employed as radio maintenance officers. For the most part they lived on gun sites and were responsible for the day to day maintenance, fault finding and repair of instruments, which often had to be carried out under battle conditions. During the high speed fighter-bomber raids of the winter of 1942–43, when London streets were littered with small pieces of silver paper dropped by the enemy, several ATS radio maintenance officers with small parties of ATS telecommunication mechanics toured London gun and searchlight sites to modify radar equipment to combat this radio interference. If to clear the faults necessitated the removal of a part of the equipment, a new part was fitted on the site and the faulty one sent back to workshops, where it was frequently repaired by ATS tradeswomen.

BIBLIOGRAPHY

Batt, Reg. 1991. The Radar Army. Winning the War of the Air.

Budiri, Robert. 1997. The Invention that changed the World. Publisher Little Brown and Company.

Campbell, D'Arn. April 1993. Women in Combat. Journal of military history, volume 57. Issue 2.

Dobinson, Colin. 2001. AA Command. Methuen.

Gilbert, Martin. 1990. Second World War. Fontana.

Gordon, Brig. Sandy, DDME, HQ AA Comd Oct 53–Oct55. "REME in AA Command".

Grenfell, Joyce. 1993. "Joyce by Herself" (Chapter "Wishes for a Godchild"). Publisher ISIS.

Hogg, Ian V. 2002. Anti Aircraft Artillery. Publishers Crowwood Press.

Hogg, Ian V. 1978. Anti Aircraft. A History of air defence. Publishers (London) MacDonald and Jones.

Jeans, Sir James. 1943. "Physics and Philosophy". Cambridge University Press.

Jones, R. V. Most Secret War. 1978. Hamilton.

Millington, Major M. S. F., OBE, TD. "The Women Who Served the Guns".

Pile, Sir Frederick. "Ack-Ack Command". 1949. Publishers Harrap.

Price, Alfred, "Skies of Fire". 2002. Cassel and Co.

Pritchard, David. 1989. "The Radar War. Germany's Pioneering".

Smith, Michael. "Station X". 1998. Macmillan Channel 4 Books.

Women's Royal Army Corps. (Pages 130 132)

Also available in ISIS Large Print:

On and Off the Flight Deck

Henry "Hank" Adlam

"We had seen enough now to know that we would be lucky, either one of us, to see the end of the war and the future was always a taboo subject with any of us."

Hank Adlam began his naval flying career in January 1941 when he entered the flying course at Gosport naval barracks. Subsequently, on completion of flying training at Netheravon, he was selected as a fighter pilot and moved to the fighter school at Yeovilton. He took part in operations against the enemy from two Escort Carriers and one Fleet Carrier in the Atlantic, Arctic, Mediterranean and Far Eastern theatres of war. He went on to fly in operations against the Japanese in 1945, helping with the American battle for Okinawa.

His book is not about heroes and leaders of naval air warfare, although he points out that there were many of them, but a portrayal of an average young man, anxious to fight for his country, but having to cope with the tension of warfare.

ISBN 978-0-7531-9494-2 (hb)
ISBN 978-0-7531-9495-9 (pb)

Bugle Boy

Len Chester

"Sleeping on a straw-filled palliasse was like lying on the back of a hedgehog. But nothing had prepared me for day one."

From the day he went to his elder brother's Kings' Squad Parade at Chatham in 1937, all Len Chester wanted was to become a bugler/drummer boy. Two years later, when he was 14, he did just that and joined the Royal Marines.

He tells of life on board HMS Iron Duke in the dangerous waters of Scapa Flow and then on the Arctic convoys to Russia, how he learned the many bugle calls, and of playing at the funerals of men when he had never been to a funeral before. Len Chester survived the war and came home. At Remembrance Day parades he wears the rare off-white beret to which only men from the Arctic Convoys are entitled — yellow-white because blood turns yellow when frozen in snow.

ISBN 978-0-7531-9486-7 (hb)
ISBN 978-0-7531-9487-4 (pb)